THE Warm AND Welcome HOME

Quin Sherrer

Regal

From Gospel Light
Ventura, California, U.S.A.

Published by Regal Books
Gospel Light
Ventura, California, U.S.A.
Printed in the U.S.A.

Regal Books is a ministry of Gospel Light, an evangelical Christian publisher dedicated to serving the local church. We believe God's vision for Gospel Light is to provide church leaders with biblical, user-friendly materials that will help them evangelize, disciple and minister to children, youth and families.

It is our prayer that this Regal book will help you discover biblical truth for your own life and help you meet the needs of others. May God richly bless you.

For a free catalog of resources from Regal Books/Gospel Light, please call your Christian supplier or contact us at 1-800-4-GOSPEL or www.regalbooks.com.

Library of Congress Cataloging-in-Publication Data
Sherrer, Quin.
    The warm and welcome home/Quin Sherrer
    p. cm.
    ISBN 0-8307-2905-4
    1. Hospitality—Religious aspects—Christianity. I. Title.

BV4647.H67 S555 2002
241'.671—dc21   2001048861

1 2 3 4 5 6 7 8 9 10 11 12 13 14 15 / 09 08 07 06 05 04 03 02

Rights for publishing this book in other languages are contracted by Gospel Light Worldwide, the international nonprofit ministry of Gospel Light. Gospel Light Worldwide also provides publishing and technical assistance to international publishers dedicated to producing Sunday School and Vacation Bible School curricula and books in the languages of the world. For additional information, visit www.gospellightworldwide.org; write to Gospel Light Worldwide, P.O. Box 3875, Ventura, CA 93006; or send an e-mail to info@gospellightworldwide.org.

Contents

Foreword

During my 38 years of marriage to Jamie Buckingham, our home was always open to others. Jamie—the generous and loving man that he was—was forever inviting someone to come visit us, whether it was another minister and his family, a missionary back in the States on furlough or a young single mother and her children with no place else to go. Jamie believed in following the directive of Paul in Romans 12:13: "Share with God's people who are in need. Practice hospitality."

I will be honest with you. Sometimes being hospitable was not easy. Sometimes it was downright inconvenient. I remember getting weary once and complaining to God, to Jamie and to anyone else within earshot that I was tired of having so much company. Then the Lord led me to read Matthew 10:41: "Anyone who receives a prophet because he is a prophet will receive a prophet's reward."

Talk about motivation! Over the years Jamie and I received many servants of God into our home. Boldly, I began to claim for myself every reward that was laid up for them!

It was not always easy to prepare big meals, change bedsheets, wash extra loads of towels and otherwise have my normal routine turned upside down at the ring of a doorbell. But the act of inviting outsiders in—of being hospitable—reaped joys and rewards I would never have known if I hadn't opened that door.

I learned early on, fortunately—for it probably saved my sanity—that my family did not necessarily have to do a whole lot when company came. With Jamie's help, I learned that all we had to do was be ourselves and our visitors would take us as we were. When someone came to our home, we would say, "Make yourself at home. Become part of the family while you are here." That always made our guests feel comfortable. And it took a load of responsibility off of me.

My five children—now grown and with children of their own—were real troupers. They had more opportunities than most kids to learn the lessons and the joys of giving and sharing. I could not begin to count the number of times Jamie and I asked them to give up their bedrooms and bunk in with one another in order to make room for "a few extra."

But each of them learned to love our visitors as much as Jamie and I did—especially the missionaries. The children would sit in wonder and awe as they listened to the most amazing real-life bedtime stories—tales of planes filled with Bibles flying over the jungle, of faraway tribesmen laying down their weapons to hear more about Jesus, and of "God's smugglers" courageously crossing over Communist borders to share the Good News. The richness of those contacts has had a profound impact on their lives. Their own efforts to be hospitable today are now having an impact on a third generation of Buckinghams.

I believe hospitality is not only a gift but also a mandate that we as Christians should practice. "Love one another," (John 13:34) the Bible says. John makes plain that when we love one another, we are showing our love for God. When we are serving others, we are serving God (see John 13:20).

My good friend, Quin, with sensitivity led by the Holy Spirit, has included in this volume all the facets involved in Christ-centered hospitality. In addition to gaining an understanding of the spiritual implications and rewards of being hospitable, you will find a lot of good, practical advice on how to make your house a home—one that is open to serving God's people, whether they are relatives, friends or strangers. I encourage you to take her suggestions to heart. After all, who knows when you may have an opportunity to entertain "angels unawares" (Heb. 13:2, *KJV*).

Jackie Buckingham
Palm Bay, Florida

Acknowledgments

My appreciation to my former pastor, Rev. Peter Lord, of Park Avenue Baptist Church, Titusville, Florida, who gave me permission to quote freely from two booklets I wrote for his church in the late 1970s: *Let's Practice Hospitality* and *Decorating Our Homes to Please the Lord*. I also appreciate his dedication in teaching seven couples in my home every Sunday evening for six years, encouraging us not only to be hospitable but also to become disciplined in our Christian lives. He and his wife, Johnnie, were such wonderful examples to me, as well as encouraging cheerleaders. They still are, though we are separated by many miles.

I want to express my appreciation to Regal Books for material quoted from my books published with them; and I especially thank Deena Davis for her editorial expertise on this book project. I thank Servant Publications for permission to quote from books I've written for them, including portions excerpted here from A *House of Many Blessings*, which I coauthored with Laura Watson.

And my eternal gratitude to Mary Jo Looney, Lib Parker, Elizabeth Mizell, Barbara Eddings and Laura Watson—those long-ago friends who helped me develop the gift of hospitality and who still stay in touch, sharing God's love.

Special thanks to Ruthanne Garlock and Fran Ewing who have provided me a home away from home to write on many occasions and have always been such gracious hostesses, showering me with hospitality.

And to Aunt Nell Moore, Miss Hospitality herself!

Finally, to our Lord Jesus Christ, who helps us make a house a home!

Introduction

Share with God's people. . . . Practice hospitality.
ROMANS 12:13

Practice hospitality. If the thought causes fear in your heart, don't panic. Hospitality doesn't mean you must have a perfectly appointed home, be a gourmet cook or know every social grace in an encyclopedia of etiquette. Extending hospitality is a matter of simply reaching out to those God puts in your path. And as you practice, the art of hospitality gets easier and easier!

For years I longed for a book like the one you are holding in your hand. I wanted a handbook that would

- show me how to properly set the table;
- give me creative and inexpensive ways to decorate;
- give guidelines on how to treat my overnight guests;
- offer hints for being more hospitable to speakers at our women's meetings;
- explain how I could mentor someone younger;
- help me find a way to balance giving with receiving;
- explore what the Bible says about hospitality.

If you, too, have questions about some of these things, this book is for you. In it I have shared my own rocky road to learning, as well as stories from other women—some of whom mentored me. The appendix is designed for individual or group Bible study. Don't miss this important section of the book.

You will also find dozens of practical pointers to adapt to almost any situation—whether you live alone or with others, have a large or small family, are rich in material possessions or have a limited income.

When we begin to realize that a Christian's material possessions are gifts from God to be used for His purposes, we are off on an exciting adventure. As we cooperate with Him, we allow the Lord to use us, our homes and our possessions in creative ways we may never have considered before.

Ask the Lord to make your house into a home of many blessings—a refuge, a sanctuary, a haven—where His love is extended to others.

May your home be a place where the people who enter your door feel accepted, welcomed and loved.

Quin Sherrer
Colorado Springs, Colorado

CHAPTER ONE

A Welcoming Home

[The Lord] blesses the home of the righteous.

PROVERBS 3:33

How I wish I had known at an early age how to accept my house, no matter what. For years I was embarrassed to tears to let anyone see where we lived.

I clearly remember the Christmas night when I helped LeRoy, my husband of one hour, pack all our earthly belongings. Hospitality was the last thing on my mind as we crammed our wedding presents and a few of LeRoy's Air Force duds, along with my suitcases, into the back of his old green car. We were striking out from Florida for engineering college, our honeymoon just stopovers on the way.

Something inside me shouted all the way to Houston, "Whoopee, only one man to feed!" I couldn't imagine what it would be like to sit across the table from just one man—for a lifetime. Almost heaven, I thought.

For 10 years my mother had operated a boarding house in Tallahassee, Florida, to help support and educate her four children, of whom I was the oldest. She served family style (all you could eat for 75 cents) each day in her dining room and fed more than 300 people—college boys, construction crews and state legislature workers.

My, how they could eat! "Shove the potatoes down this way, man," someone would call. "Don't hog the rolls," another would shout to the person seated at the far end of one of the long tables. I watched in unending amazement as they devoured bowls heaped high with corn on the cob, pole beans, black-eyed peas, new potatoes and yellow squash, and Southern fried chicken, baked ham or succulent roast beef slices piled high on platters. Hot yeast rolls—my mother's special recipe—brought fresh from the ovens by the dozens, were smothered in butter and cane syrup. My sister and I were the waitresses, constantly on demand to refill tea glasses and replenish the food bowls. After a while I grew to dislike the job immensely.

I resolved that when I married, cooking for one man would be a snap. I certainly didn't want to be bothered with having a bunch of people at my dining table.

It hadn't yet occurred to me that I hadn't even learned to cook. I had tried often enough. My mother's main kitchen helper, lovingly called Big Cook, would shoo me away from her stove whenever I'd peep over her ample shoulder to watch how she made her pineapple delight. But later she'd shout, "Get on out of here now," and hand me a bowl full of the creamy pineapple custard. "You'll have plenty of time to learn to cook when you marry. Besides, honey, you won't be cooking for 300 men."

Five days after our wedding, LeRoy and I arrived in Houston and moved into a tiny off-campus walk-up apartment with mismatched overstuffed furniture and limp curtains.

Some weeks later I shouted at LeRoy, "I hate this apartment! I dearly hate it," and then hurled a pillow against the wall near where he sat studying at a rusty old fold-up aluminum table. When the pillow hit, a bit of the sea-green wallpaper flaked off and floated down to the bare floor.

"Hush! The landlady downstairs will hear you," he warned, leaning over to retrieve the pillow. "Shouting won't fix anything, anyway."

"I hope she does hear me," I replied. "For what she's charging us, she could afford to fix up this place. I don't see how she can expect anyone to live in this dump."

Within six months I was already longing for my mother's old house back in Florida. But I was stuck. My only hope was that as soon as LeRoy got his engineering degree we could leave. In the meantime, both of us had to work to pay for his tuition and this horrid apartment. I was glad it was a temporary dwelling. Surely not my home.

But the six months we had planned on living there dragged into two and a half long years. I never lifted a finger to make those dreary rooms attractive—to make it a real home. I invited only one couple from the university to come over to eat with us.

Though I had studied cookbooks and experimented with recipes designed for a shoestring budget, I still doubted my ability to cook a "company" meal. I had good reason to doubt; it seemed that every time I used the pressure cooker, it blew up. LeRoy would help me scrape carrots, spinach and even bits of stewed chicken off the kitchen ceiling and walls whenever the cooker blew its relief valve. If we had company for dinner, they might discover my kitchen clumsiness!

After LeRoy finished school, he accepted a job in Florida at the Kennedy Space Center. It was a booming area with housing as scarce as gold nuggets. Over the next several years we lived in a succession of dwellings—a postage-stamp-sized trailer, a cottage that the owner boasted she'd converted from a chicken coop, and box-style houses in various subdivision tracts.

CREATIVE HOSPITALITY

All this time I called myself a Christian, yet it never crossed my mind to ask Jesus how I could turn a chicken coop into a haven for my family. I was still pining for a dream house—one I could invite friends to share with us. In my mind's eye it was a four-bedroom, three-bath, ranch-style brick house surrounded by lots of trees for our three youngsters to climb. But this dream was both impractical and out of reach.

Then one day I stumbled onto a way to be hospitable. We attended a church that was forming for the first time. After the service everyone stood around getting acquainted. A young woman named Lib Parker, whom I'd discovered was just my age, said to me, "I wonder if you'd like to go home and get your Sunday dinner and bring it to our house. I know this is unusual, but we don't have enough for two families. I just think it would be great if our families could get to know one another."

I turned to LeRoy, and he answered for us, "Why not? Sounds like fun!"

So we went to Lib and Gene's house that Sunday. The next Sunday they brought their four sons to our house along with their dinner. During the following year we combined our Sunday dinners often, either at their small house or ours. Sometimes we picnicked at a lake nearby. The children played outdoors on swings in warm weather and huddled indoors over board games during the cooler winter months. Lib and I became long-time prayer partners, and our children always felt they had four Parker brothers.

A CHANGED PERSPECTIVE

Before long it dawned on me that I just might be able to adjust to my limitations and make better use of what we had in our home. Though I was still shy around people, I yearned to open my heart and home to others. If I could do it for Lib's family, couldn't I do it for others as well?

Though I was still shy around people, I yearned to open my heart and home to others.

The art of hospitality comes naturally to some women. It didn't for me. It took me so long to feel comfortable around others. I focused on all my "have-nots," never accepting any of my God-given "haves." I had to learn that it's not so much what I cook on a limited budget but that I prepare it with love.

I saw another perspective one morning when I was reading the Old Testament. Excitement raced through my heart when I read what God told His children living in exile:

Build houses and settle down; plant gardens and eat what they produce. Also, seek the peace and prosperity of the city to which I have carried you into exile. Pray to the LORD for it, because if it prospers, you too will prosper (Jer. 29:5,7).

Why, I was God's child! Even if I felt I was living in exile, I should act like my home was permanent. I resolved to treat my home with more imagination and love and to share it with others. I asked God to show me how.

CHRIST AT HOME WHERE I LIVE

The lessons were long and hard before I got my perspective completely straightened out. I knew that the more Christ was at home in my heart, the more He would be at home in my home. Right? That meant I'd be glad to walk with Him through every room of my house and have Him sit at my table. I wouldn't be ashamed for Him to open any closet or listen in on our suppertime table talk. I'd be thrilled for Him to see into every nook and cranny of the home I had lovingly made into a refuge for my family.

Invite Him to open my cluttered closet? Invite Him to eat any meal I cooked? Are you kidding?

Lib gave me a plaque that read "Christ the unseen guest at our table." Sometimes I regretted that I had hung it on our kitchen wall. It made me ask myself too many penetrating questions: Was the conversation at our table pleasing to Him? Did I spend too much of meal time fussing at the children or correcting them? Or maybe even passing on some gossip? Or complaining instead of counting my blessings?

My attitude began to change when I turned again to the Scriptures. In Luke 10:38 I found that Jesus enjoyed going to Bethany "where a woman named Martha opened her home to him." I'm sure it wasn't always convenient for her, especially when He came with 12 hungry men who also tagged along! But I believe Jesus was more at home in Bethany among His friends Martha, Mary and their brother, Lazarus, than almost anywhere else. He apparently stayed with them whenever He was in the area.

A good portion of Jesus' ministry was home centered. On more than 20 occasions Jesus participated in a meal or told a parable related to a mealtime experience. He said to a chief tax collector, "Zacchaeus, come down immediately. I must stay at your house today" (Luke 19:5). When He went to Peter's home for supper, Jesus healed Peter's mother-in-law of a fever, then she got up and served Him (see Luke 4:38-39). Jesus enjoyed a wedding in Cana, a feast at Levi's and a banquet at Simon's house (see John 2:1-2; Luke 5:27-29; Luke 7:36). I like to imagine Him throwing the first "dinner on the grounds" party when He invited more than 5,000 to stay while He multiplied five fish and two loaves collected from a little boy—He fed the whole crowd (see John 6:9-13). Have you ever thought about the lad's mother who packed his lunch and also taught him to share? I have, because that's a facet of hospitality.

FAMILY FIRST

Consider the significance of mealtime. Dr. Paul Mickey comments:

> The dinner table is the traditional symbol and practical center of family togetherness. It is the place where we eat, talk, relax, and enjoy the company of those we love most. . . . Every mealtime is a time of giving and receiving, serving and being served.[1]

I remember how I learned a valuable lesson about the people I should honor most in my service of hospitality. We had finally moved into our first home with a dining room. I had quit my job as a newspaper reporter and turned a small space off the kitchen into an office where I wrote articles for several Christian magazines. One afternoon, my 10-year-old son, Keith, hurried by my desk on his way to the kitchen for a drink. Seeing a magazine with my byline on an article, he stopped and picked it up. "By Quin Sherrer, homemaker," he read aloud.

"Mom, I didn't know you were a homemaker," he said, looking me in the eye. "I just thought you were a writer."

"A writer? Not a homemaker? Oh . . . Keith!" After he left I fell sobbing across my typewriter.

Lord, show me how to let my family know I really am a homemaker and that they are the priority in my life, I prayed.

I immediately headed for the kitchen to start supper and prepared something special to each family member. Later, when it was time to eat, there was a starched tablecloth on the dining-room table, and candles were lit. The meal looked pretty inviting—hot steaming bowls of chicken, mashed potatoes and all the trimmings.

"Who's coming for dinner, Mom?" Sherry asked.

"You are! Just our family," I said, encouraging them to take their seats. "God showed me today—through Keith—that I haven't let you know that you are more important to me than any company we'll ever have at this table. I am sorry I haven't let you know you hold first place. We're going to eat here every night from now on."

I noticed that as we ate at the dining-room table night after night, with a nice cloth and candles on the table, we lingered longer and longer to talk and to laugh and enjoy one another's company.

How different it was from the suppers I served them in the kitchen, on a plastic tablecloth! In the past I had reserved the dining room for "company" meals. But after all, who had God given me who was more important than my family? No one. Absolutely no one! My family seemed to genuinely appreciate my special care. Even today, when any of our six small grandchildren come for a meal, I set the table with a cloth, and I light the candles. They love it.

Did you know that after the destruction of the Temple the home took on a special significance?

> The dinner table of the home became, as it were, the altar of the Temple . . . the table was to be consecrated. It was to be a place where more than food was to be passed; it was also to be set apart, that the words of the Torah might be exchanged. . . . Around the table, the family sang songs . . . the father instructed his family in the words of Torah. It was a place to celebrate holidays and festivals with joy and dedication.[2]

Wherever you live, I want to encourage you to accept your home—no matter what the circumstances—as the place God has provided for you and your family during this time in your life. And I challenge you, as I challenge myself, to make mealtime a special time for all who gather at your table to eat and share.

In what ways could you let your family know how special they are to you? (Examples: Write a letter. Leave a note of encouragement on their pillows. Cook a special meal.)

Why not pause right now and thank God for the place He has given you to live? Accept your home and give it back to Him to do with as He pleases. Ask Him to release His flow of creativity in you through your home as you use it to serve God, your family and all those He will send your way.

I have had a special plaque hanging in my kitchen for years. Its words represent the principles my family holds most dear.

God Made Us a Family
We need one another.
We love one another.
We forgive one another.
We work together.
We play together.
We worship together.
Together we use God's Word.
Together we grow in Christ.
Together we love all men.
Together we serve our God.
Together we hope for heaven.
These are our hopes and ideals;
Help us to attain them, O God;
Through Jesus Christ our Lord, Amen.[3]

Notes

1. Paul A. Mickey with William Proctor, *Charisma* magazine (March 1986), p. 75, reprint from their book *Tough Marriage* (NY: William Morrow & Co., 1986).
2. Marvin R. Wilson, *Our Father Abraham* (Grand Rapids, MI: Eerdmans, 1989), p. 215.
3. The words on my plaque are "The Christian Family Standard," adopted by the Family Life Committee of the Lutheran Church, Missouri Synod.

CHAPTER TWO

A Dream House on a Tight Budget

Unless the LORD builds the house, its builders labor in vain.

PSALM 127:1

"Say, your living room really has potential," Mary Jo Looney, a grandmother with a pixie smile, said as her gaze roamed across our living room. I had just finished teaching an informal Christian writing course at my house.

"What do you mean?" I asked. I had met Mary Jo only once before, but I'd heard she had a flair for decorating on a shoestring budget.

"Oh, if your furniture were arranged differently, you'd be able to seat more people."

LeRoy and I had moved and reshuffled our den and living-room furniture many times, so we could accommodate up to 20 people who met twice a week for our Bible studies. But our current arrangement was the best possible, we thought.

Mary Jo offered to bring some friends from her church over to give our house a face-lift. Her stipulation: my husband had to agree. With his permission, I invited her to come back for the house makeover.

What did I need to do to get ready? Nothing, evidently; but I asked my prayer partner, Lib, to be there when this bevy of strangers invaded my home to do heaven-knows-what. The night before they came, I barely slept, worrying over whether I'd made a big mistake by giving Mary Jo carte blanche with my house. What if I didn't like what she did? What if I was really uncomfortable with the results?

Mary Jo had told me on the phone that God had already supplied what I would need for our home. She said most women have accessories hidden in their closet, attic or garage or under the bed. Those were the places she would look.

Not if I could help it! I didn't want her clawing through my closets, let alone the garage. So I rummaged through things myself and pulled out all the extras I thought she might use, piling them on the picnic table in our screened porch. Besides, it would save her time—as well as me embarrassment.

On Thursday morning, Mary Jo arrived at the front door wearing a carpenter's apron complete with hammer and nails. She carried dried flowers and a large staple gun. Trailing behind her were four women I had never met. "Meet our team," Mary Jo said, calling off their names. "Now, for decorating day—D-Day, we'll call it."

She asked Lib and me to sit in the living room with them as they prayed before getting started on the renovation. "Lord, may Your creative gifts flow through each of us so that we may decorate this home to Your glory. May it reflect the personality of the family who lives here—not our own individual tastes. Lord, we just want to make it an even more inviting place for Quin's family and all others that will come. Give us Your strength and joy as we work together. When we leave, may even more of Your peace pervade this home. We thank You for the privilege of helping each other and using the various talents You have given us. In Jesus' name, amen."

After the prayer we all headed upstairs to the master bedroom. "Mary Jo," I protested, "you told me you would rearrange our living room, so we could seat more people. Why in the world are you going to the master bedroom first?"

"Because the master bedroom should be the prettiest in the house. That's the sanctuary for you and your husband—it's where the king and queen reside. Now get busy and clear this clutter. Throw out these old magazines and other stuff you don't really need every day. Go down to your living room and bring me the most gorgeous bric-a-brac you have there."

"But you promised me the living room would—"

"By the end of the day you will see that the living room will also look good," Mary Jo assured me, "but this room where you and LeRoy spend your time together must be the most attractive, not just a room full of leftovers." She made a shooing motion with her hands and I went downstairs to find something to bring back to the bedroom.

While she and a couple of her friends rearranged the furniture upstairs, another friend, Margaret, was busy making curtains from printed sheets for our bedroom windows.

Our oldest daughter, Quinett, who was taking sewing in high school, helped Margaret sew up curtains for her own bedroom windows from pink-and-blue flowered sheets. Margaret showed her how to use the heavy-duty staple gun to cover the wall behind her bed with matching sheet fabric. It looked better than any fancy wallpaper.

Keith's room was made over in a blue theme, and I told my son he could paint a surfing scene across one whole wall that weekend.

Sherry's room was redone in flowered yellow sheets—curtains, bedspread, lampshade, canopy over the bed and covering for one wall all in matching fabric. My youngest daughter was thrilled.

Meantime I kept busy polishing old brass pieces Mary Jo wanted for wall decorations and running up and down the stairs to deliver supplies to various ones who called for help. Once in a while I'd peek in to see how Mary Jo and Lib were doing in whatever room they were working.

It was a good thing I'd committed this day's activities to the Lord, or I'd have been upset when I saw them switching furniture from room to room. But I remembered our prayer that morning, and I knew God was using His creativity in each woman.

I could hardly believe the great new look they were creating, using *what we already had* to better advantage. In fact, they were capturing our family's personality in the minute details, even in what they chose to use in wall groupings, from family pictures to my grandmother's old china plate from England.

I had often complained about our old furniture as "those awful hand-me-downs," since much of what we owned were relatives' castoffs or used-furniture-store bargains. But now, in their new places near windows, those wonderful old wood grains shone as the sunlight bounced off them.

Mary Jo was true to her promise in the living room. When she rearranged the couch, chairs and end tables, we had more than ample room for our Bible study crowd. LeRoy was so pleased he asked, "Does she rearrange garages, too?"

Late that night, as I collapsed in bed, tired but happy, I thought back over the day. I recognized that no matter where I would ever move again—to a walk-up flat, a crude beach cottage or a cabin in the woods—it would be home. Our spot. Our place to express our likes, tastes and personalities.

General Suggestions

Mary Jo has trained over 65 women in her church, and together they have redecorated more than 1,000 homes free of charge. She strongly believes in sharing what you don't need. Anything that isn't needed after a house's transformation, is recycled. It goes into Mary Jo's "goody van," because the next home she goes into may need that very lamp or bedspread or those curtains. The first time Mary Jo came to my house, she shared a list of suggestions.

- If you need a buffet server in the dining room, consider moving a long dresser from a bedroom to the dining area. After all, a chest is a chest is a chest. Use it where you need it most. If you move it from a bedroom, it might provide room for a chair or desk in that bedroom.
- Don't hang pictures too high. Eye level is best. Hang pictures and mirrors off center and use groupings over couches and beds. Don't be afraid to experiment. If you goof and need to hide a small

nail hole in the wall, toothpaste will cover it.

- Give a personal touch to the hallway by hanging family portraits there.
- Frame Scripture verses, postcards and unusual greeting cards for wall decor. Mary Jo believes in putting Scripture verse plaques in every room of the house. "Change them often in the bathroom—you have a captive audience there, and kids will memorize them painlessly."
- Paint a family tree (literally a tree, with trunk and graceful branches). Hang framed family pictures on them.
- Hang a small picture inside built-in bookcases.
- Put chairs in bedrooms, so people have a place to read or visit. If the room is large enough, group two chairs with a small table and lamp for a sitting-room effect. This is especially good for the master bedroom.
- A dust ruffle sewn to a fitted sheet keeps the ruffle from sliding offcenter.
- Cover window shades: cut fabric that coordinates with the bedspread to fit and then glue on with spray adhesive.
- Make curtain tiebacks from ribbon, yarn, boat rope, chains, braids, beads or a contrasting fabric ruffle.
- Make headboards out of anything interesting. One of our friends made a headboard for their king-size bed from an old archway of a building that was being demolished.

- Marbleize a tabletop by painting it a cream color; let dry. Wipe a coat of oil-based stain across it and then lay a sheet of saran wrap on top; lift off immediately and you have instant marble!
- Don't be afraid to mix periods of furniture. Most pieces will blend harmoniously if you don't go overboard.
- Make matching bedspread and curtains from decorative sheets. Staple sheets on a wall behind your bed for an interesting and colorful effect.
- Sew lace doilies or hankies onto solid-color toss pillows. This looks especially elegant on a velvet pillow.
- Keep glass, silver and brass clean and polished. It reflects light and creates an atmosphere of warmth. Use rubbing alcohol to clean glass, chrome and the shower stall—alcohol even removes black shoe polish from carpet!
- Dried flowers or weeds look great in tall or small baskets, and they keep indefinitely. However, be sure to spray weeds with a bug killer before bringing them indoors. To keep weeds from shedding, spray with hair spray.
- A live potted plant, a dry arrangement or silk flowers in each room (including bathrooms) will bring subtle colors of nature into your home.

Your home can be a place of your dreams only if you're willing to put yourself into it. But how fulfilling it is when you hear your family and friends say, "I feel comfortable in this place."

CLUTTER BLINDNESS

In time, Mary Jo taught a class on homemaking to the women of the church. She started the class with a stunning question: "Are you the best housekeeper you know how to be?" Then she opened her Bible and read, "And whatever you do, whether in word or deed, do it all in the name of the Lord Jesus, giving thanks to God the Father through him" (Col. 3:17).

The women were still squirming when she made another appalling statement: "God sees into closets, too!"

I didn't like that! *I'm just not neat,* I thought to myself. But I kept listening as she said, "God is a God of order, not confusion, and everything should be kept in its proper place. Look at how beautifully and orderly He made the universe. He wants our homes to reflect the same order He puts in nature—He wants them organized and attractive.

"We can get so wrapped up in habit that we're blinded by clutter," Mary Jo said. "I'm sure none of you leaves your ironing board piled so high with clothes that your husband has to step over it to get into bed. None of you parks your vacuum cleaner in the living room and lets it stay there for decoration." She raised her eyebrows.

Some women giggled, identifying their own poor housekeeping habits.

Mary Jo said she didn't blame some husbands for not wanting to come home to a messy house or having to side-step the ironing board left up in the master bedroom. She then gave us a list of suggestions to live by:

- The master bedroom should be the prettiest in the house—keep it picked up and orderly. If you aren't married, still make your bedroom the most attractive place possible, because you want to create order and peace in the decor of your special place.
- The children's room(s) should be next in importance. Make your children feel special. Help them pick colors, wall hangings and some Scripture plaques. Spend money on good mattresses for them.
- The dining room or kitchen is next in importance, because that's where the family sits to eat and enjoy family fellowship.
- Have a special "hubby" corner for your husband if you are married—his place to feel at home.
- The living room, or whatever room is used when company comes, is lower on the priority list because family comes first. But it is still important because by its orderliness it witnesses to others your commitment to God.
- Go through each room and ask yourself, *Is Jesus pleased with this room*? If not, discard the things you wouldn't want Him to see. Is anything in disorder? Rearrange the room.

- Keep the house clutter-free. Get rid of outdated catalogs, old magazines, shoes and clothes that don't fit. Remember this Scripture: "A time to keep and a time to throw away" (Eccles. 3:6).
- Go through the house one room at a time and do a thorough job of setting right each room before going on to the next. Set a goal: one chest of drawers today, one closet tomorrow, one bookcase the next day. It will overwhelm and discourage you if you try to do too much at one time.
- At night, before going to bed, straighten your living room and kitchen. What a relief to come to breakfast without having to face a mess!

If you're thinking, *What does decorating have to do with hospitality?* reflect for a moment. Don't you feel more comfortable having others come to your home when it is picked up and orderly? Before we can be hospitable, we have to feel at home where we live.

Before we can be hospitable, we have to feel at home where we live.

Vivian Hall, in her book *Be My Guest,* says that hospitality is easier when we live by these simple rules:

- Decide on the lifestyle that is best for your family and live accordingly.
- Live within your means. Finances, time and energy are limited commodities, so do not overextend yourself in a desire to make a good impression.
- Be adaptable.
- Eliminate competition from your relationships with other people. Seek to gain the approval of God and not of men.[1]

To her list I would add: Be yourself! Each of us is unique, with varying gifts and personalities. Let your home reflect your personality. Decorate with the things you treasure and build from there.

You will no doubt be troubled by thoughts like, *If I could just get a new chair . . . or sofa . . . or table . . . or. . . .* That may well be the only way to pull your room together. However, look first at the purpose of hospitality, then at the possibility of making do with what you have. You may be surprised at what is at hand.

God-Honoring Decor

When I realized everything I have is God's, I began to do some soul searching. If my home was His, did I have it—and myself—arranged to please Him, as well as my family?

One of the things I learned from Mary Jo was that the entryway should exalt Jesus so that all who entered would know He lived there too. One day, when our paperboy came to collect his fee, he said, "Why is your manger scene sitting out here in August?"

"Because it reminds me that God sent His Son into the world to show us what God is like. Do you know Jesus?" I asked him.

The manger scene had provided a perfect opportunity for witnessing. So now I leave it on the hall table year round.

CHRISTIAN SYMBOLS

Christian symbols used to turn me off. When I entered a home and saw a profusion of plaster plaques, something inside me would churn. I wasn't walking with Jesus then and didn't know the significance of the emblems.

When I came to understand their meaning, I realized our home could be tastefully decorated with emblems of our faith without splashing the walls and coffee table with cheap objets d'art. I also wanted to guard against a hodge-podge effect.

I'm sure there are some people who still don't care for symbolism, perhaps fearing it borders on idolatry. Yet our Christian faith is rich in symbolism. Jesus referred to Himself as the Bread of Life, the Light of the World, the True Vine (see John 6:35; 8:12; 15:1).

Of all Christian symbols, the cross is perhaps the most universally accepted today. More than 400 shapes are in existence, including the Latin, Greek, Jerusalem, Celtic and Maltese.

At an art show, LeRoy and I found our first decorative piece that expressed our faith—a handcrafted bronze-and-wood plaque with a cross superimposed over a fish and the word "Savior" engraved underneath. We hung it inside our front entrance. That empty cross constantly reminds us of a Savior who conquered death and now lives in heaven to intercede for us.

Not only did we want to reflect the Lord Jesus through decorative objects in our home, but we also asked Him to show us what we needed to remove from our home. "Lord Jesus, is there anything in here that is an abomination to You? Anything that's connected with the occult or the demonic realm?"

We got rid of several questionable wall hangings when missionary friends told us of their true significance.

God's warning to the Israelites is just as appropriate for us today: "The images of their gods you are to burn in the fire. Do not covet the silver and gold on them, and do not take it for yourselves, or you will be ensnared by it. . . . Do not bring a detestable thing into your house. Utterly abhor and detest it" (Deut. 7:25-26).

Protect your home by getting rid of any of Satan's counterfeit guises that give glory to violence. Remove from your house and destroy any pornography, New Age or occult toys, games, music, videos, disks, books, posters or any artifacts associated with false religions, cults or occult practices. Pray over your family members at night—ask for health and safety—even if you do it after they are asleep.[2]

A PEACE HOME

Scripture says, "My people will live in peaceful dwelling places, in secure homes, in undisturbed places of rest" (Isa. 32:18). One of the things LeRoy and I did early on after we dedicated our lives to the Lord was to dedicate our home by way of a blessing ceremony.

The word "blessing" conveys the idea of invoking God's favor upon, bestowing happiness or prosperity, guarding or protecting." That was exactly what we wanted—God's blessing.

Dedication ceremonies with appropriate speeches were common in Israel's history. For instance, Psalm 30 is a song sung at the dedication of the house of David. In Deuteronomy 20:5, the question is asked, "Has anyone built a new house and not dedicated it?" as though this was an expected action. And of course the dedication of the house of God was celebrated with joy. Read about it in Ezra 6:16.

In Judaism, one of the most important family values is a peaceful home—*shalom bayit*. Jesus taught, "Blessed are the peacemakers" (Matt. 5:12) and Paul said peace is one of the fruit of the Spirit (see Gal. 5:22). A Christian home, then, should be a peaceful home. *Shalom bayit.*

Jesus told His disciples when they went into a town or village to search for a worthy person and stay at his house. "As you enter the home, give it your greeting. If the home is deserving, let your peace rest on it" (Matt. 10:12-13).

LeRoy and I wanted our home to have that peace. When we learned that our friend Forrest Mobley, an

Episcopal priest, was coming through town, we asked him to lead in our house dedication. Kneeling at the coffee table in our living room, we acknowledged God's ownership of our home while Forrest recited a house-blessing prayer:

> Let the almighty power of the Holy God be present
> in this place to banish from it every unclean spirit,
> to cleanse it from every residue of evil and to make
> it a secure habitation for those who dwell in it; in
> the name of Jesus Christ our Lord.

We went from room to room as he prayed in each one and then asked God's blessing on those who would use or occupy that room. Just before he left, Forrest added what I later called his postscript prayer:

> And now, Lord, use this house for Your glory and
> this family to love others to You.

I never dreamed that soon after those prayers were said I would be sleeping 11 people on pallets on the living room floor while 7 others slumbered upstairs. Or that God would send as many as 96 people in one week to our house—some to eat, some to fellowship and some to stay overnight.

LeRoy and I have moved into several dwellings since Forrest Mobley blessed our home 30 years ago. But in each house or apartment, we have had a dedication ceremony with a few close friends gathered, even if there wasn't a minister to preside over it.

You may want to have a house blessing for your home, too. Make it a special occasion, even if you don't have the pastor there or even if the house isn't new but only because you have never actually dedicated it to the Lord. One thing I can guarantee: You will be blessed; all who enter will be blessed; and God will be glorified.

Notes

1. Helga Henry, foreword to Vivian Hall, *Be My Guest* (Chicago: Moody Press, 1979), p. 9.
2. Quin Sherrer and Ruthanne Garlock, *A Woman's Guide to Breaking Bondages* (Ann Arbor, MI: Servant Publications, 1994), p. 172.

CHAPTER THREE

A Balance Between Giving and Receiving

Therefore receive one another, just as Christ also
received us, to the glory of God.

ROMANS 15:7, *NKJV*

We were all taught that it is more blessed to give than to receive, but somehow in our spiritual thinking we have internalized only part of the equation. We need to find the balance between giving and receiving.

And why do we resist receiving? Is it because we feel unworthy? Of course we are. But Jesus died for us, so He considers us more precious than His own life. If we don't receive Jesus, there really isn't any meaning in giving presents to others as a celebration of His birth.

One reason I can open my home so freely to others now is because I've learned to ask for help. The first time I had 40 people come for supper, I thought I could handle it. However, I soon found that idea ridiculous. I called Lib, and she came running over—in her bedroom slippers. Many times since then, when I would have a big party, Lib would be in the kitchen making the punch or replenishing the sandwiches. I called her my Martha.

MY BIGGEST LESSON

Let me tell you how I learned my biggest lesson in the area of receiving.

Our family of five had just sat down at the dining-room table for supper when the doorbell rang.

"I'll get it," 12-year-old Keith said, dashing to the door.

He came back slowly, carefully carrying a bouquet of pastel spring flowers. He handed me the accompanying card. I glanced at LeRoy, who was trying to hide a smug smile.

"With love from your sweetheart, LeRoy," I read aloud.

"Wow! Dad must have done something awful!" Keith said. "Flowers? For no special occasion, Mom?"

"That's right, honey. But aren't they pretty?"

Fifteen years earlier, on our first anniversary, LeRoy had sent me a dozen red roses. But no flowers since then. What had he done? What had I done? Why flowers?

The next night as we sat down to eat, LeRoy slipped a brightly wrapped present beside my plate. Surprised, I opened it to find a new nightgown. A love note was tucked into its folds.

The following evening he offered to do the dishes. The next night he volunteered to vacuum the downstairs. Since he was not accustomed to doing either, I brushed him off. "Are you kidding? Go read your newspaper. This is my job."

"On Friday night I'd like to take you to Sandpiper's, the finest seafood restaurant on the East Coast," he said firmly. "Be ready at six, dressed in your best."

"But it's the end of the month," I sputtered. "You know perfectly well we don't have enough money left to eat there. We can't possibly afford it!"

"Be ready. I'm taking my bride out for the night of her life."

The next morning I phoned my prayer partner, Lib. "LeRoy is acting strange," I said. "I wonder if I have reason to suspect him of something. I mean, he never offers to vacuum or to wash dishes. And he sent flowers and gave me a gift for no particular reason. I tell you, something is fishy . . ."

"Oh, it's just a midlife crisis!" Lib offered. No help at all.

On Saturday night I dressed in my best pink chiffon and reluctantly got in the car with LeRoy. En route to the restaurant he explained he had a tool he must return to James England. He motioned toward the gadget on the seat between us.

When we arrived at the Englands's house, he said, "Honey, get out and go in with me. Just for a minute."

"No way. The pastor's car is in the driveway. He's probably stopped by to pray with them. You know Ann is still in bed flat on her back, trying not to miscarry again."

"Come on. Please! Come on in just for a moment," LeRoy insisted.

I got out and walked up to the front door with LeRoy, who was clutching the tool in his hand. He pressed the doorbell.

When James flung open the door I could see a huge banner on the wall behind him that read "WIVES, WE APPRECIATE YOU!"

In the next room I could see Pastor Lord and his wife, Johnnie, watching. We all exploded in laughter. They told me that each of the seven husbands in our couples' group, which Pastor Lord taught on Sunday evenings at our home, had agreed to surprise his wife that week with flowers, a nightgown and offers to help around the house.

Now the men were cooking us a scrumptious charcoal-grilled steak supper. Festive tables were set up in the dining and living rooms, complete with linen tablecloths and soft candlelight. Violinists had been hired to serenade us while we ate. The setting was far superior to the Sandpiper, and the food was certainly more delectable. One couple took their plates to join Ann and James in the bedroom since Ann couldn't leave the bed.

After dinner we played games and laughed uproariously. But our hilarity calmed considerably when Pastor Lord called timeout for his weekly Questions and Answers. Actually, it was his "report card" time, since he graded us each week on how well we had learned any lesson God was trying to teach us.

"What did you think when your husbands surprised you with gifts and offers to help?" he asked the wives. "How did you react? Were you a loving *receiver?*"

Each wife painfully agreed she deserved a big fat F when it came to receiving graciously from her husband. We'd all been highly suspicious. Extremely poor receivers.

I came away from that evening determined to be a good receiver. I had always found it easier to give than to receive, so I knew I would have to ponder this lesson. God said He "loves a cheerful giver" and that "it is more blessed to give than to receive" (2 Cor. 9:7; Acts 20:35). But He also said, "Freely you have received, freely give" (Matt. 10:8). I also remembered the verse, "Give, and it shall be given unto you; good measure, pressed down, and shaken together, and running over, shall men give into your bosom" (Luke 6:38, *KJV*).

RECIPROCAL LIVING

I learned to find pleasure in doing for others and giving to and surprising others. But I wasn't prepared to be on the receiving end. The night of our wives' appreciation dinner I finally understood that if my husband or my friends wanted to give to me, I was robbing them of a blessing by my negative attitude that said "No, thank you. I don't need your gifts, talents, help." At the same time, God was saying to me, "You are robbing yourself of the restorative quality of receiving."

We are made in such a way that we cannot be fulfilled by giving alone; we must also receive.

We are made in such a way that we cannot be fulfilled by giving alone; we must also receive or we will soon be depleted and our desire to give will become superficial. We cannot give out of emptiness. On the other hand, taking but never releasing results in a stagnant state of being.

Keep in mind that receiving honors the giver; refusal to receive denies his personhood.

When LeRoy and I became a part Pastor Lord's congregation, we soon learned that members were encouraged to register their abilities at the church office and were expected to volunteer to help one another. I registered to teach writing classes. LeRoy offered to help the young men learn how to repair their cars on Saturdays in our side yard. Giving and receiving.

When our 13-year-old daughter Sherry wanted to learn to bake bread, I called the church office and found that Margaret Broward had offered to teach this. So Sherry and I spent one Saturday in Margaret's kitchen as she taught us to mix, knead and bake. We left with several loaves of delicious homemade bread.

The Bible is full of reciprocal living commands— more than 50 of them, to be exact. These are sometimes called the "one anothers." Pray for one another. Love one another. Receive one another. Use hospitality to one another.

Both Peter and Paul had something to say about this.

Peter wrote, "God has given each of you some special abilities; be sure to use them to help each other, passing on to others God's many kinds of blessings" (1 Pet. 4:10, TLB). Paul told the Ephesians: "Why is it that he gives us these special abilities to do certain things best? It is that God's people will be equipped to do better work for him, building up the church, the body of Christ, to a position of strength and maturity" (Eph. 4:12, TLB).

Every member of the Body of Christ has a unique God-given ability and ministry that are essential for the upbuilding of others. The purpose of reciprocal living is that believers enable one another in Christian living and thus demonstrate together the love and unity that should characterize God's people.

SURPRISE BLESSINGS

When we began taking young people into our home, a minister told us, "God will bless you." But I wasn't looking for any spectacular out-of-the-ordinary happening.

Then about six weeks later, LeRoy came in from work with a wide grin on his face and a blue check in his hand. "Guess what, honey?" he said. "You are going to get a new kitchen for Christmas—at least a new oven and flooring for this room. See this?"

"What are you talking about? Where did you get that check?" I asked, sitting down on the boot bench to take in this sudden news.

"Well, you know each year they give special awards at work. I told the men in our carpool months ago that if I ever got one, it would be a miracle of God. I never expected it to happen. But look—a miracle in my hand!"

You can say LeRoy's company gave us that money. And you would be right. But I believe God let them channel His money to us through that award—the first my husband had ever received in his 20 years with the company. Yes, God gave me a new floor that takes less time to clean and a new oven, so I could cook better meals. I firmly believe that what the minister told us came true. God poured out His blessings beyond measure after we received someone into our home in Jesus' name, without thought of receiving in return.

PRECIOUS GIFTS

The Bible reveals that hospitable folk receive blessings galore without expecting anything. When Abraham and Sarah received the three strangers at Mamre and offered them food, the Lord revealed through them that Sarah would have a son (see Gen. 18:1-14).

Boaz offered bread and grain to Ruth and got a wife in return; and from their heir came Jesus (see Ruth 2:14-20; 4:13-22).

Though Abigail's husband, Nabal, was rich, he was an ill-mannered, selfish drunkard. She, on the other hand, was beautiful, intelligent and hospitable.

Saul was still on a rampage, seeking to kill David and his band of men—for David had already been anointed king by the prophet Samuel. During sheep-shearing time, when David and his men were hiding from Saul, David sent word to the wealthy Nabal, asking for food. David's men reminded Nabal's men that they had served as a wall of protection around Nabal's huge flock of sheep and goats while out in the fields near Carmel. But Nabal refused the future King David his bread, water and meat.

When Abigail heard that her husband had declined to offer hospitality, she took off on a donkey caravan to feed David's entourage. Sending her young men ahead, she met David on the way. Not only was she bearing food, but she was also on an even more serious mission. Appealing to David's conscience, she asked him not to kill her husband and bring reproach upon David's own life (see 1 Sam. 25: 2-28).

When Elijah, God's servant, asked the impoverished widow of Zarephath for water and bread at the moment she was using her last bit of flour and oil for her son and herself, she fed Elijah first. Then her bowl of flour and jar of oil never ran out during the long drought that followed (see 1 Kings 17:7-24).

When the prominent woman of Shunem and her husband built Elisha a room to stay in and gave him food, she was rewarded with the birth of a son (see 2 Kings 4:8-37).

When the two travelers to Emmaus invited the stranger walking on the road with them to stay for the night, Jesus made Himself known to them during the breaking of the bread (see Luke 24:13-32).

Look how Mary and Martha were blessed by having Jesus in their home. When their brother, Lazarus, died, Jesus came to Bethany to raise him from the grave and to reveal some of His greatest truths: "I am the resurrection and the life" (see John 11:21-27).

Who can ever forget the story of the resurrected Jesus cooking breakfast over a charcoal fire for His disciples? When the disciples in their boats looked toward the shore, they saw Him there, frying fish for them. "Now come and have some breakfast," He called to them. Then He, the Son of God, went around serving them bread and fish (see John 21:5-13).

And what of the disciples who had denied, deserted and failed Jesus? They got a blessing that has reverberated throughout time. For in these precious intimate moments they saw Him for who He really is: the resurrected Lord, Son of God, Prince of Peace.

Jesus was both a giver and a receiver. He gave of Himself in the serving. But He also received in welcoming His men—those friends who had failed Him. He, the *giver* and the *receiver*, wants us to do the same.

The balance between giving and receiving requires tempering mercy with wisdom, or else a show of love will simply degenerate into sentimentality. In each situation we need God's wisdom to be able to see through His eyes. Then the love we give others will be God's love, and no one can resist that!

CHAPTER FOUR

Open-Door
Blessings

*Is not this the kind of fasting I have chosen: to loose the chains
of injustice and untie the cords of the yoke, to set the oppressed free and break
every yoke? Is it not to share your food with the hungry and to provide the
poor wanderer with shelter—when you see the naked, to clothe him, and not
to turn away from your own flesh and blood?*

ISAIAH 58:6-7

Are you ready for whoever comes to your house?

In Luke 22, we read about preparation for the Passover. It was the custom of the inhabitants of Jerusalem to receive Passover celebrants as brothers. They furnished space in rooms or apartments where travelers might eat the feast. So the disciples asked Jesus if there was a particular house where He wanted them to prepare the Passover meal. Jesus told them they would see a man who carried a pitcher of water and to follow him to the chosen house.

Makes me wonder about the others involved—those in the background. To begin with, it was unusual to see a man carrying water—that was women's work. Did the man with the pitcher know someone would be looking for him? Not likely. Did the householder know who would be using his house's upper room? No. But Jesus knew, and He knew how to find the right place.

What a blessing to be of service to Jesus like this, and for what a purpose—His last meal in the Old Covenant with His disciples! Although there was no way for the householder to have known the importance of what took place that night, he was ready for whoever came to his house.

Are you so in tune with Jesus that He could send anyone to your door—even someone difficult? Are you prepared to serve others? Are you willing to remain in the background? To cook food and wash dishes? To watch the baby while your guests spend the day at the beach? To make beds or lend the car?

We need to ask ourselves these hard questions if we determine to follow Jesus' call to service. He said that if we serve even the least of our brothers we are serving Him, whether we realize it or not. (see Matt. 25:37-40). If we would be ready to serve Jesus at all times, then hospitality must become a way of life for us.

Whenever we express hospitality through our homes, we can be sure we are on safe scriptural ground. Even a casual reading of the Old Testament impresses us with the way those folk showered hospitality on friends and strangers. Gracious hosts not only fed and provided overnight lodging for guests—as they did for Jesus and the disciples during Passover—but they often cared for the servants and animals of their guests as well.

In the New Testament we also read about believers enjoying food and fellowship with each other: "Breaking bread from house to house, they were taking their meals together *with gladness and sincerity of heart*" (Acts 2:46, *NASB*, emphasis added). Whether it was a simple meal or a feast, whenever God's people got together, they worshiped the Lord and enjoyed fellowship with one another.

One Sunday night our church members celebrated our own feast following a day of fasting. We called it "A Feast of Homes." Some 1,500 of us gathered in 64 different homes, in family units, to enjoy a meal, to worship and to partake of the Lord's Supper.

Thirty-four people brought food to our house. After we had enjoyed a leisurely meal, we moved to the living room, where our leader read from the Bible and led us in holy Communion. Some of the children, sitting on the floor, began to sing as we broke the loaf of home-baked bread, symbolizing the broken body of Christ.

I closed my eyes to concentrate on the joyful songs of praise in piping children's voices. My heart was touched as I thought this could have been a New Testament church commemorating the death of Christ—right here in our home.

When the cup of juice was passed, I wondered if it hadn't been much like this not long after Pentecost when those new Christians continually were "devoting themselves to the apostles' *teaching* and to *fellowship*, to the *breaking of bread* and to *prayer*" (Acts 2:42, *NASB*, emphasis added).

BEING AVAILABLE

One Sunday after church, my youngest daughter, Sherry, then a teenager, asked me, "How many are coming for dinner today?"

"You can set four extra plates," I replied. "Daddy invited some visitors to come eat with us."

"Why, Mom?" she asked, as she opened the silverware drawer. "Why do we *always* have company on Sunday?"

"Well, it's one way we can share Jesus' love. Those people drove a long way to attend our church. Daddy wanted to bring them home to eat with us so that he could have more time to talk with them about the Lord."

Handing her the dinner plates, I shuddered a moment, remembering all those years I'd neglected to invite people into our home, even LeRoy's friends from work. I had begun my hospitality journey the day Lib and Gene invited us home for Sunday dinner and we reciprocated the next week. It was a start. But I really got liberated the day I read something from Paul's letters in *The Living Bible*: "You should practice tenderhearted mercy and kindness to others. Don't worry about making a good impression on them" (Col. 3:12).

I finally understood that all Jesus required of me was to be available to share His love with others.

What freedom that gave me! I could be myself. I finally understood that all Jesus required of me was to be available to share His love with others.

SHARE THE BLESSINGS

Over the years I have talked with mature Christian women who were willing to share their hospitality hints with me. Here are a few of those suggestions.

- Prayer: We saturate our home with prayer before our invited guests arrive. Usually my husband and

I pray together, asking God to express His love through us. We also pray that our guests will feel the presence and the peace of the Lord in our home.

- Music: We play Christian music softly on the stereo as guests arrive, helping to create an atmosphere of praise.

- Greeting: When people come to our home for the first time, we welcome them with a smile, handshake or hug—but always warmly. When I introduce people, I try to find a mutual point of contact, so they can find an immediate point of conversation. I'll say something like "You have something in common—both of you are excellent seamstresses." Or "Joe just moved here from Miami—I know you used to live there, too, Malcolm." I try to have a listening heart and seek out guests who are lonely and get them to talk. We need to follow the example of Jesus and be careful how we listen.

- Blessing: If we have too many people for all to sit at the dining table, we gather in the living room and stand in a circle and hold hands while LeRoy offers the thanksgiving prayer. Then we go to various tables I've set up in our downstairs rooms. When we entertain business associates, even if they are not Christians, we always say the blessing before the meal. After all, the Lord is our provider and we want to thank Him.

- Cohost: When we are having a large group of people over, I like to ask a cohost to assist me. We can take turns working in the kitchen.
- Leftovers: We pray while we prepare the meal, asking God to make it nourishing and attractive. Sometimes we have to pray that He will show us how to stretch the food to feed a few extra people. We try not to be wasteful. After Jesus fed the 5,000, He had the disciples gather up the fragments. I have learned to save leftovers to use in soups, salads or casseroles. Rather than throwing out coffee or iced tea, we freeze it and save it for punch. We use leftover bread to make bread crumbs for casseroles.
- Preparation: Preparation ahead of time is vital. During the years we were in Peter Lord's church, where company every Sunday was routine, I spent preparation time in the kitchen every Saturday. Then on Sunday, with table already set and the food only needing to be warmed, we could sit down to a meal without a lot of fanfare in the kitchen.
- Extra Food: I find it helpful to keep extras in the pantry for unexpected guests—cans of beans to add to a pot of chili, tuna to add to boiled eggs and relish for a quick lunch, extra bread in the freezer, packages of instant pudding, lots of rice and potatoes.

I have learned many creative ways to prepare dishes with one deboned boiled chicken—from a

Chinese chow mein dish to a Mexican tortilla chip concoction. And I'm sure you too can feed up to 20 on one chicken if you use some creativity.

- Recipes and Records: Keep an indexed file of favorite recipes, sorted according to beverages, desserts, meat dishes, salads and vegetables. I also try to keep a record of what I have served to whom and when, so I can vary the menu when I have some of the guests back again.

- Hot Drinks: In winter I no longer serve fresh-perked coffee. Instead, I fill a 36-cup coffeemaker with water and plug it in. Guests are invited to make their own hot drinks using the instant mixes I set out—herb teas, cocoa, mocha or coffee. I have much less waste now.

- Helping Husband: My husband is a marvelous host at the door, greeting guests and making them feel truly welcome. When our house buzzes with guests who've come for a late supper, he's often in the kitchen helping refill an empty punch bowl while I replace sandwiches; or he's off in a corner talking to a bashful soul who is lost around lively talkers.

- Apologies: Never apologize for how the house looks if company comes in unexpectedly. I try to keep our house "picked up," so it looks orderly. But if it isn't spotlessly clean, I don't want to draw attention to it by saying "Oh, my house is a mess and I haven't gotten the bathrooms cleaned yet."

Try to remember that guests have come to see you, not your house, and you want to be gracious to all your guests—especially to those who pay you the honor of dropping in unannounced.

- Teenaged Hosts: When our children were teenagers, we let them invite their friends for Sunday dinner. They liked to offer the invitation, help cook the meal and then assist in serving. Afterward we all sat in the living room and visited. It helped us get to know our children's friends better and gave our youngsters a chance to practice hospitality.

- Strangers: We often invite college kids home after church for a meal. When our own children were in college far from home, a family's invitation to them to enjoy a home-cooked meal was greatly appreciated; so we reciprocated by doing the same for lonely youth in our community.

- Great Legacy: One of the greatest heritages we can give our children is to have them share our table with great men and women of God. I don't mean we invite all the guest pastors or missionaries home to eat after they've spoken at our church. But we do ask the little widow who depends on God for every need, the schoolteacher who has spent her life joyfully caring for her aged mother, or the retiree who has served God in the factory where he's worked all his life.

ADD SOME VARIETY

Here are more tips to make even the most casual meal fun. The various types of parties mentioned below may be adaptable to your situation.

- Brown Bag Lunch: These are sometimes called "poor boy" suppers. Everyone brings a sack lunch. Guests sit out under the trees and eat picnic style. In case of rain, they move into the living room and sit on the floor, listening to music. The host usually furnishes the beverage.
- Spur of the Moment: Don't hesitate to ask another family to bring their Sunday dinner and combine it with yours. Some of the greatest fellowship I can remember have been at dinners when two or more families combined their meals at a home, a park or at the beach.
- Glory Party: These sessions are sometimes called "prayer and praise" parties because they are held to praise the Lord. They include much singing, from old-time favorites to Scripture choruses. A guitarist is an asset. If you have percussion instruments such as tambourines, triangles, maracas or cymbals, let each guest choose one and encourage them to make a joyful noise unto the Lord. After a time of singing and prayer, serve light refreshments.
- Count It All Joy: When you are experiencing trials, throw a "joy party." This is a time when you least

feel like celebrating. But James 1:2 (*KJV*) tells us to "count it all joy" when we go through testings. Invite some of your closest friends over for a backyard picnic. You'll be surprised how you will be lifted up after these Christians have prayed for you and shared your burden.

• Dessert Party: Invite friends over after supper for dessert. You can furnish the food or ask the guests to bring their favorite home-baked goodies, perhaps with the recipe to share. Or ask everyone to bring fresh fruit. This is a good mixer party for newcomers or to get acquainted with neighbors.

In the years since I started seating our family in the dining room amid candlelight, a host of others have joined our buffet suppers. It hasn't been unusual to have anywhere from 45 to 60 people in our home each week—some for prayer meetings, others for meals, still others just to talk and snack.

Jesus is setting me free to be more flexible in some of my attitudes. Now when an invited guest asks "What can I bring?" I'm likely to say "What would you like to bring?" I've found that most people have a favorite dish they like to cook; and if they ask, they are serious in their offer to bring some food. So I let them. Since learning the hard lesson that hospitality is a two-way street—receiving as well as giving—I want to use this "talent" to the fullest. We learn to use our gifts by practicing them.

When you are acting in God's will, the blessings of open-house hospitality will come upon you in showers too wonderful to measure. And you begin to see that loving others is what hospitality is all about anyway—because we need each other.

CHAPTER FIVE

Keepers of the Inn

*Cheerfully share your home with those who need a meal or
a place to stay for the night.*

1 PETER 4:9, *TLB*

Finding a cat shut up in my suitcase or a child dumping the contents of my purse no longer surprises me. When I travel to speaking engagements, staying in private homes has helped me learn to appreciate a good bed and meal but not get terribly upset when the unexpected happens.

I do remember a time, though, when I almost lost my cool.

My friend Ginger and I had been on the road three hours to reach a modern split-level farmhouse. Weary from four hours of speaking at a women's seminar earlier in the day, I had looked forward to collapsing in bed, even without supper.

When I rang the doorbell, the wife, husband and children all met us at the door. They just stood staring at us. Finally the wife spoke.

"Sorry, but I'm not ready for houseguests yet. Could you just come back later when I'm more organized?"

"Sure, we'll go into town and eat. Then I'll call you from there," I said, trying hard to smile. "But would you care if we just checked into a motel? I don't mind taking care of the expense," I offered.

"Absolutely not. What would the women on our executive board think of me if you did that?" she replied.

Two hours later we returned. She told us we could sleep in the bed her son shared with his dog. She didn't change the sheets or make up his crumpled bed. Reluctantly he came in and removed his hamster cage from beside the bed. Two beach towels were all we could find in the linen closet for our baths.

The next morning our hostess admitted we were her first houseguests. She had volunteered her home because it was new and she was an officer in the women's group where I was to speak. Thinking back to our own hospitality goofs, we laughed with her about her uneasiness and assured her we were flexible and forgiving.

However, this experience did make me more conscious of seeing that my own houseguests are provided with essentials to make their stay more comfortable.

DEALING WITH SURPRISE

On another speaking trip, when Ginger drove me, we were housed in a large rambling two-story home. Spacious and tastefully decorated, it featured a bath complete with jacuzzi, shower and commodious dressing room. I insisted that Ginger pamper herself in those facilities since she'd driven for the past 12 hours. Then, too, our hostess said there were other bathrooms down the hall.

That night when I sank into a tub of warm water in one of the smaller bathrooms, I was puzzled over the gritty sand on the bottom. Lathering up, I noticed the soap had a peculiar smell. When I spied the dish of food and water beside the tub, I realized I was sitting in the dog's bathtub and was covered in flea soap.

"The dog's bathroom! Are you kidding me?" Ginger asked when I admitted my blunder while we were loading the car to leave the next day.

"So much for letting you have the best bathroom," I laughed as we drove away. "I wonder what our hostess thought when she discovered I'd even used Muffy's towel when I was a 'guest' in his canine tub?"

I've slept in upstairs attic rooms in Holland and Germany, and in a basement room next door to a noisy boiler in Brooklyn.

In one home there was no closet space in the room given to me because 10 years earlier the family's teenage son had stored his car parts there. The shell of the old car still sat abandoned in the carport.

I have also stayed in places that made me positively purr with contentment. Once on a Georgia plantation I was given a bell to ring for a uniformed housekeeper to bring me breakfast in bed! But far more often I've stayed in ordinary homes with kids and friendly husbands who welcomed me because they'd learned to share what they have as part of their Christian hospitality.

Why do I stay in homes instead of motels? Because most times the organizations that invite me don't always have funds for accommodations. And I've been pleased to form long-time friendships and stay with families on repeated visits. Some have even become "adopted" families to me.

But now I must admit that as I've grown older, I've come to really appreciate the privacy of a hotel when I don't know the family well. Today I need more rest simply to be refreshed in body and spirit for the next morning's speaking engagement.

HOSTING A GUEST SPEAKER

As Christian women, we may all have the opportunity at one time or another to host people who come to our churches as guests—missionaries on furlough, women's ministry speakers, seminar leaders, etc. I have been on both the receiving and the giving end of hosting. From my personal experiences as a guest speaker and from interviewing missionaries, pastors, speakers and other guests who stay in private homes, here are suggestions that cover the basics of making a guest speaker's stay more comfortable.

- Mail in advance details about your guest's speaking engagement—when and where the meeting will be. If the guest is driving, include a map and explicit directions. Provide a telephone number that the speaker can leave with family members back home for emergencies while he or she is with your group.
- Tell the speaker where he or she will be met at the plane terminal (the baggage-claim area is a good choice) and who to look for (it's a good idea to have the party meeting the speaker hold a sign with the speaker's name on it).
- Be on time when a speaker arrives in town—whether it's by plane, bus or car.
- If the speaker brings a prayer partner, also take care of the prayer partner's room, meals and so forth.

- Have someone assigned to your speaker to care for his or her needs at the meeting—getting water, showing where the restroom is, providing a shield if a lot of people want to interact with him or her before the meeting begins. Have a quiet place in mind if the speaker wants to find a place to pray.

- In the room where the speaker is staying overnight (whether a hotel or a private home), provide some fresh fruit, some juice and a carafe of water. Some speakers appreciate a snack when they arrive at their room. It's always thoughtful to include a basket with an assortment of traveler's necessities: hand cream, shampoo, shower cap, extra toothbrush, breath mints, aspirin are some of the items my guests have needed on occasion.

- If the speaker is staying in your home, you may want to give others the pleasure of providing meals for you as their act of hospitality. But be sensitive. Several times I have had to wait until 10 P.M.—my time—to eat with a host's family; and due to the time-zone change, I was much too tired to enjoy either their company or the food.

- Even if you don't drink coffee, have it available for your guest's breakfast. I once stayed in a beautiful new home where the hostess ate all her meals out. I had to wait until I arrived at the 10:00 A.M. meeting before I could get anything beyond water.

- Send the speaker a note of thanks after he or she gets home, mentioning some things the speaker said that touched you or others in the audience. Don't hand the speaker a note of thanks and an honorarium check before he or she speaks—an unfortunate mistake many hostesses make.

BEING FLEXIBLE

JoAnne, wife of a military doctor, says that if you have guests in your home, flexibility will save you from unnecessary trauma. She adds: "Make plans, but always be willing to change them. Once when we were stationed with the Air Force in Germany, I had 15 people show up at our house to stay for several days. It wasn't unusual to get a call from the train station in Wiesbaden from someone saying a Christian family somewhere had told them our house would be a good stopover. We would set up pallets on the floor for the children and put the adults in beds. Sometimes George and I would go next door to our neighbor's house to sleep, so a couple could have our master bedroom."

From her experiences, JoAnne offers these tips:

- Put good mattresses in your guest room.
- Esteem others more highly than yourself. See things from their perspective when planning meals and arranging the guest room.
- Pray over the guest room—that the guest will find peace and rest there. You might want to leave some

Christian reading material on the bedside table.

- If you are hosting a guest speaker, allow him or her freedom to study and prepare without having to spend all free time with your family members.
- On the other hand, if you are a guest speaker staying in a home and the meeting goes on until late at night, don't expect the hostess to serve you a hot meal at midnight. It is better to communicate in advance what your schedule will be and discuss what the hostess will have available and when, than to have misunderstandings later.
- Provide good, balanced meals, not just what is easy for you to make (one guest speaker was served a similar chicken and broccoli casserole at five different homes).

HOSTING THOSE WITH SPECIAL NEEDS

Fran, a nurse, has been married for over 40 years to her doctor husband, Mike. As a result of polio, he has been in a wheelchair all their married life. Fran gave me some tips for considering houseguests with varied special needs:

- Ask if there are any special things needed to make your guest more comfortable.
- Take up scatter rugs, so a wheelchair will move more easily across the floor or so the elderly won't trip.

- Put a mat in the tub to prevent slipping.
- Put a night-light in the bedroom and bathroom.
- If a guest is diabetic, know what food he or she needs and the times the he or she needs to eat.
- Leave room at the table for a wheelchair, even if you have to rearrange some of the furniture.

SETTING THE MOOD

While most people like to feel at home when in another's house, it is up to the hostess or host to make them feel welcome. Fresh flowers are a nice welcoming touch. If nothing is blooming in your yard, most grocery stores sell cut flowers. This makes guests feel that you care about the details of the visit and were looking forward to their arrival.

Fresh flowers are a nice touch that make guests feel you care about the details of the visit and have looked forward to their arrival.

My friend and often-coauthor, Ruthanne Garlock, points out that "hospitality is a spiritual trait; entertainment is a worldly concept based on pride and greed." Ruthanne and her husband, John, a former college professor and now international speaker, have stayed in homes literally around the world. She has learned a lot about the need for being hospitable wherever she hangs her hat.

"Flexibility will save you from unnecessary trauma," Ruthanne says. "I'm learning to be sensitive to the Lord's voice when things seem to go awry, to get His perspective on the situation.

"There is a difference between entertaining guests and hospitality. No matter what your budget, you can make people feel welcome in your home by giving thought to their comfort." For guests who have traveled some to get to your home, Ruthanne shares her hints for making travel-weary guests feel more at home:

- As soon as your guests arrive, show them their quarters and let them deposit their suitcases.
- Show them where the bathroom is and tell them if they will be sharing it with others (teens, small children or adults). Show them where to find the towels and washcloths.
- Provide space in their closet for hanging travel bags, and provide a few extra hangers.
- Provide water and glasses for the bedroom.
- Offer fruit juice or something refreshing when guests arrive.
- Let guests use laundry facilities or offer to wash their clothes for them. Show them where the iron and ironing board are kept.

- The guest room should be arranged with a place for the suitcase—preferably not on the floor, if possible.
- In the bathroom, provide a hand mirror and wastebasket, towels, washcloths, soap and toilet tissue (you would be surprised how many of these items are missing, even in American homes).
- Provide a mirror and a lamp of some kind in the guest room.
- Keep pets and children out of the guest's room (dog won't lie on bed, cat won't dig in suitcase, kids won't explore the contents of luggage, etc.).
- Try to avoid awkward situations—like a teenaged son popping into the bedroom in the morning to get his clothes while a guest is still asleep.
- Take time to make guests feel they are not imposing.
- Respect your guests' privacy. Don't play your radio or TV so loudly that guests can't sleep, pray or study. For the sake of privacy don't put your guest on a sleeper couch in the family room, if possible.

Once when Ruthanne and I were rooming together in another country as invited speakers, our accommodations were very limited, almost primitive by American standards. Looking around at the have-nots was easy. But we began to laugh at our circumstances and make up little praise songs for what we did have. "Thank You, Lord, for this nail on the wall—we can hang a mirror to see how to comb our hair."

We went through the rest of the trip looking for ways to be thankful, knowing we were privileged to speak to these women who were probably attending the first conference in their lives.

Ruthanne continues to laugh about some of her experiences, especially those when she stayed with families who did not speak English. She always takes gifts to a family's children, which is a hit in any language.

"I want to be a blessing, not a burden, when I am a houseguest," she says. "I do appreciate any extra effort the family makes for my comfort, and I've learned from them the warmth of special touches. Now I often put a bowl of fruit in the guest room when people stay in our home."

Making Do with What You Have

The Lord may ask each of us to use our homes in different ways. JoAnne and her Air Force physician husband have moved a lot. Her house is furnished with what she calls "joyful junk." But every item reflects Jesus, from the stained-glass window from Germany to a kneeling bench from an ancient church. She gives us some hospitality tips from her varied experiences:

- Sometimes when you feed the multitudes, you must put your hand on the pot and ask God to multiply and bless it!

- My philosophy: Do with what you have. If you have some of the finest china and silver and linen, use it. If not, improvise. If you don't have silver pieces for your table, use lots of baskets. If you don't have flowers, gather sticks, rocks and leaves and make a centerpiece. Put rustic with rustic and fine with fine. But do use cloth napkins—they are quick and easy to iron. They say "I care and you are special to me."
- It takes time to be hospitable. Be rested and dressed when company comes. I prepare food ahead of time; but if I have a last-minute salad to put together, I'm not intimidated if women gather in the kitchen to watch me. If I'm comfortable, they will be comfortable. That means, don't attempt anything that is a burden to you—keep the menu simple. Whatever you feel good making is what you should serve.

Whenever I walk through JoAnne's front door, the house signals "Welcome!" JoAnne told me, "I spend a lot of time in prayer in my house, and it should reflect that. Whenever I expect company, I want them to feel I have prepared a place for them. Jesus has gone to prepare a place for us, so I treat my guests as if they were Him when I prepare a place for them in my home."

I once saw a wall plaque that said "Let All Guests Be Received As Christ." This is a wonderful principle to live by in our roles as innkeepers to the guests who will grace our homes.

CHAPTER SIX

Angels and Strangers

Practice hospitality to one another (those of the household of faith). [Be hospitable, be a lover of strangers, with brotherly affection for the unknown guests, the foreigners, the poor, and all others who come your way who are of Christ's body.] And [in each instance] do it ungrudgingly (cordially and graciously, without complaining) but as representing Him.

1 PETER 4:9, AMP

I was hurrying to finish the magazine article I was writing on hospitality and resented the interruption of the phone.

"Hi, Quin. This is Sue," an unfamiliar voice said. "We are vacationing in Florida and just can't wait to see you. We're down at McDonald's. Wonder if you could meet us and let us follow you to your house, so we could visit?"

"How will I know you—I mean, recognize you, Sue?" I stammered, fishing for a clue.

"There are four of us. I'll be behind the wheel of the yellow Cadillac with Texas license plates."

"Give me 10 minutes." I prayed under my breath, "Lord, I don't have time for this interruption, and I sure don't have time for hospitality right now. Help!"

Thirty minutes later, as we sat in our den sipping iced tea, I studied Sue's face. She must be LeRoy's cousin, I decided. Blond hair, blue eyes—fits with all his German kin back in Texas.

This woman knew everything about us. Yet to me she was a complete stranger. She even knew the NASA department where LeRoy worked as an engineer at Kennedy Space Center.

When LeRoy came in from work moments later and saw our four guests, he arched his eyebrows at me. I shrugged my shoulders. He didn't know them either!

When the smell of chili simmering on the stove wafted into the room, Sue hinted that it must really taste good. I invited them to stay for supper and then ran to the kitchen to dump three more cans of beans into the chili pot and to make a large tossed salad. When our children and my mom joined us, we had 10 around the table.

As we talked, I discovered they were now considering staying overnight with us. Inside I was more than irritated. I had that magazine article on hospitality to finish and mail by tomorrow. Though our home had been open to others for years, tonight I just didn't have time for hospitality—especially to strangers!

After supper Sue asked LeRoy to help them find some oranges and grapefruit they could pick. He took them down to Mother's backyard with several empty grocery sacks. I stayed home to clean up the kitchen and change bed linens. An hour later he came back alone, saying they'd decided to drive on a couple more hours that night and then stop at a motel.

"Did you ever find out who Sue is and how she knew so much personal information about us?" I quizzed him.

"Oh, yeah. She turned out to be my mother's hairdresser back in Texas," he said, laughing.

"Hairdresser? You must be teasing me."

"No, I'm not. Don't you women tell your hairdresser *everything*?" he said, his eyes rolling. "I guess Mom talked so much about us every week, Sue became very familiar with our family."

"Familiar? That's putting it lightly!" I groaned.

God's Reward

After I crawled into bed that night, I had a long talk with the Lord. He reminded me that for years my elderly mother-in-law had not been able to comb her hair properly with her crippled, gnarled, arthritic hands. Sue, her hairdresser, had in a sense been hospitable to her in a way I couldn't, since we lived almost 800 miles away.

"Was three hours of your time and four bowls of chili given to strangers such a big sacrifice?" the Lord seemed to ask. "Didn't I promise that if you give even a cup of cold water in Jesus' name, you would be rewarded?"

"Lord, forgive me," I responded. "My attitude was rotten and my priorities were out of order." The next morning I was up at daybreak, finishing the manuscript with a whole new slant on the subject of hospitality and a fresh illustration from my own life.

GOD'S CHOICE PEOPLE

In her book *Be My Guest*, Vivian Hall explains how her family makes their guest room available to fellow Christians needing a place to stay when they are in her city. Often her guests are strangers. Yet she can think of no single instance when she had to refuse someone because of lack of room or physical strength to care for them. When you decide on this type of hospitality, this is what she says you are asking God to do for you:

- send the people of His choice;
- choose the time they should come and how long they should stay;

- protect you from people who would misuse your hospitality;
- give you spiritual insight to know how to meet both the physical and spiritual needs of your guests;
- keep your own spirit open to the blessings God has planned that you will receive from these guests;

Vivian Hall says, "I can say emphatically that God has never failed us in any of these areas. Because we have found Him so dependable, it has become more and more enjoyable to participate in the ministry of hospitality. When we have chosen to obey, our blessings have far outweighed the effort we have expended."[1]

Now when my phone or doorbell rings, rather than viewing it as an interruption, I wonder if the Lord might be sending me another opportunity to practice hospitality, even to a stranger.

The apostle John commends this attitude:

Beloved, you do faithfully whatever you do for the brethren and for strangers, who have borne witness of your love before the church. If you send them forward on their journey in a manner worthy of God, you will do well (3 John 5-6, NKJV).

Study notes on 3 John in The Spirit-Filled Life Bible state: "This letter portrays the church as a family united by bonds of love with its members extending gracious hospitality toward one another." Another note says that "those who support missionaries share in their work of the gospel."[2]

ANGELS OR STRANGERS?

Sarah, our first biblical grandmother was very hospitable; she made bread cakes for three strangers who passed her and Abraham's tent in the heat of the day. The Bible account implies that these strangers were angels. Later on in the Bible we are told, "Do not neglect to show hospitality to strangers, for by this some have entertained angels without knowing it" (Heb. 13:2, *NASB*).

I have never read that Scripture verse without thinking of an incident that happened to Marie and her pastor husband when they welcomed a stranger in tattered clothes to a picnic behind their parsonage. Marie told me about it:

It was in the evening and we had the youth fellowship from our church for a cookout in our backyard. While they were singing and having a good time, we noticed this man standing over in the shadows. I remember Charlie went over to him and invited him to come share our food and have a drink of hot chocolate. The kids were cooking hot dogs over an open fire.

The man said he didn't want anything to eat. He'd heard the singing and had come closer to hear it better. But he told me he would take a glass of cold water, if I didn't mind. The three of us—he, Charlie and I—walked back to the house.

I went in and got him a glass of water to drink. We started to walk back to the young people—Charlie walking beside him. Then it seemed we got a bit ahead of the stranger, sort of leading him to the group.

All of a sudden he wasn't there. We ran to the street and looked toward the highway that ran past our street. But he was not in sight. The street in front of our house was wide—there was no place this man could have just disappeared to in that short time. How could he walk off so quickly?

Who was this stranger to whom Marie offered a glass of cold water in Jesus' name? A tramp? An angel? Marie will never know. But she, like Sarah, was willing to share what she had with a stranger. Just a cup of cold water, given in love, is an acceptable act of hospitality, both to a guest and to God. Such a simple thing—but so worthy.

PRAYERFUL INVITATIONS

All such strangers are not angels. Some are just strangers. How do we identify the ones to whom God would have us extend hospitality? We read in the second epistle of John:

Many deceivers, who do not acknowledge Jesus Christ as coming in the flesh, have gone out into the world. Any such person is the deceiver and the antichrist. Watch out that you do not lose what you have worked for, but that you may be rewarded fully. Anyone who runs ahead and does not continue in the teaching of Christ does not have God; whoever continues in the teaching has both the Father and the Son. If anyone comes to you and does not bring this teaching, do not take him into your house or welcome him. Anyone who welcomes him shares in his wicked work (2 John 7-11).

When LeRoy and I got into the flow of hospitality, we learned we had to be careful about the people we invited into our lives, even for a brief time. I once let Mike, our first adopted son, bring home a young ex-drug addict who turned out to be a con artist. And there was the young man LeRoy tried to help who later hanged himself in jail. What spirits had we allowed into our home? Were these people God-sent or emissaries of the enemy?

We began to pray: "Lord, who do You want in our home? To whom are we to minister? To feed? To clothe? To shelter?"

Just as Jesus did nothing without first asking the Father, we must ask the Father for direction and discernment.

I once heard a pastor say, "You don't have to be the answer to every need you see. You might rob someone else of an opportunity. But if you are the one to respond, do it heartily as unto the Lord."

Old Testament hospitality guidelines were explicit: "The alien living with you must be treated as one of your native-born. Love him as yourself" (Lev. 19:34).

There may be times when God will want us to reach out in hospitality to those who cannot invite us back.

There may be times when God will want us to reach out in hospitality to those who cannot return the invitation, but this shouldn't matter. Our concerns must be to continually ask God for discernment in all situations and to be open to provide hospitality to strangers.

SINGULAR HOSPITALITY

There are some people who cannot open their homes to outside guests. Louise, a working wife whose husband will not let her have company, has found ways to be hospitable anyway. She bakes desserts for the pastor's family when they are hosting guest speakers. Once a week Louise takes a picnic or buys lunch for a coworker, so she can get better acquainted and eventually share her Christian faith.

Not all home hospitality fits into the category of couples' hospitality. Many singles don't have much money to spend on company—they suffer from financial insecurity— yet some of the most gracious hosts and hostesses I know are single and include coeds, career men and women, single parents, widows and widowers.

Janis and her two roommates often have covered-dish suppers, and they don't mind asking their friends to bring along some food. "We love to get together at our house to talk and sing and eat. It's friendship that's really important," she told me.

Once my daughter Quinett and her friend Sharona, alone one Sunday after church, decided not to let the lack of male companionship stop them from having fun. They packed a picnic basket with their very best—two china plates, two crystal goblets, two settings of sterling silverware—and set out their lunch on wicker bed trays in an exclusive garden park in Dallas. They were enjoying their salad when a woman from England stopped to talk. "What a novel idea!" the woman said. "Reminds me of the Continent." Many other people stopped by to chat with the two young women, who shared their leftovers with children who strolled by. They had a grand time! Sometimes it gives us a lift to get away from familiar settings to enjoy food, fun and fellowship.

OUR RESPONSE

When we seek the Lord's guidance, He sends a variety of people our way, each with a piece of the puzzle that will make a picture of our life's opportunity to magnify Him.

Our joy is multiplied when we share His love with those who need to feel God's healing touch, and we are doubly blessed as we minister to them. We begin to discern the pattern God is using to mold us to conform to His likeness and, like Paul, we can "give thanks in all circumstances, for this is God's will for you in Christ Jesus" (1 Thess. 5:18).

Karen Mains has said that hospitality does not seek to impress but to serve. Hospitality does everything without thought of reward, even though there is pleasure in giving, loving and serving.[3] Our churches are filled with strangers who need love. With all this in mind, a biblical response would be, "Lord, send the people of Your choice to my house." Jesus said:

> For I was hungry and you gave me something to eat, I was thirsty and you gave me something to drink, I was a stranger and you invited me in, I needed clothes and you clothed me, I was sick and you looked after me, I was in prison and you came to visit me. . . . Whatever you did for one of the least of these brothers of mine, you did for me (Matt. 25:35-36,40).

Notes

1 Vivian Hall, *Be My Guest* (Chicago: Moody, 1979), pp. 34-35.
2. Jack W. Hayford, gen. ed., *The Spirit-Filled Life Bible* (Nashville, TN: Thomas Nelson, 1991), pp. 1940, 1942.
3. Karen Burton Mains, *Open Heart, Open Home* (Elgin, IL: David C. Cook Publishing, 1976), pp. 25-26.

CHAPTER SEVEN

A Gracious Legacy

There should be no division in the body, but that the members should have the same care for one another.

1 CORINTHIANS 12:25, *NASB*

Who among us at one time or another has not had a bad moment when it comes to social etiquette?

We feel blessed when we encounter well-mannered treatment from others. But what exactly are good manners? The dictionary mentions polite social behavior. But good manners are also characterized by showing kindness, compassion and thoughtfulness toward others.

The essence of manners and graciousness is making your guests comfortable, anticipating their needs and *serving* them.

In New Testament times, the guest was greeted with a blessing of peace, kissed, had his or her feet washed and head anointed with oil, was given water to drink and served a meal.

Any stranger who entered a town at the time of Jesus was usually sure of being invited to someone's home for food and lodging. Because of the laws of hospitality, Jesus could send His disciples out, knowing they would be cared for in homes.

Although the world is different today and we are not required to invite all strangers into our homes, we do have cultural expectations that require the practice of good manners, which means treating others with respect and making them comfortable in your presence.

My generation grew up with manners drilled into us on a daily basis. But many in today's generation have not had that discipline.

American manners have been much maligned at home and abroad, but we can change that image if we consistently observe a few simple guidelines of respect for others and teach these guidelines to our children.

GOOD MANNERS

Introductions

American etiquette books tell us that when you are introducing a woman and a man, always mention the woman's name first, for you are introducing the man to the woman. When being introduced, a young man should stand. He remains standing until the women and any older men have found seats or until all who wish to sit have been offered a chair. That may sound archaic, but think about it—it's a matter of honoring women and elders.

Graciousness never goes out of style. Acceptable manners are appreciated by everyone.

When introducing your friends, find a mutual point of contact if possible, so they can begin a conversation. Say something like "You two have something in common—both of you have small children." Or "You are both from Oregon—small world!" Or "Maybe you knew Dick's brother who was on campus when you were."

Telephone Manners

It's helpful to identify yourself when you are calling: "May I please speak with Mary? This is Dot Burns from Birmingham calling."

Use wisdom about identifying yourself when *answering* your phone. One can just say "Hello" or "Good morning" or "Sherrers' residence."

Be sure your children know how to politely and properly answer the phone. One friend's daughter answered the phone and called out, "Mom, it's for you—and I think it's a salesperson." The caller, who was an important client, overhead the conversation. When my friend said "Hello," her client was clearly agitated. "No, I am not a salesperson. I called you about some business."

Moms can also set some time limits for children using the phone. Good manners include consideration of others, even of family members!

Table Manners

Gaining a basic understanding of proper table manners—an often misunderstood area of etiquette—will help us all feel more comfortable, less ill at ease and able to enjoy the food and conversation. Here are some simple tips gleaned from several experts.

- When going to the table, ladies sit first. Gentlemen, seat the lady on your right if you are in a group; then seat yourself.
- After prayer, the napkin is placed on the lap entirely open if it is lunch-sized, or in half if it is a dinner napkin. Guests wait until the hostess has taken up her napkin before placing their own. At banquets, as soon as you sit down place the napkin on your lap.

- Ladies are usually served first, but the hostess is not served first unless she is the only lady at the table.
- If the hostess is serving you, you will be served from the left and plates will be removed from the right.
- Concerning the use of utensils at your plate, the usual rule is to start with the outside piece of silverware and work toward the center.
- When eating soup, the spoon is filled with a movement away from and not toward the body. Food is taken from the side of the spoon into the mouth.
- When served meat, cut one bite of at a time; then cut another bite. When buttering bread, break off a portion, butter it and then eat it. Don't butter the whole piece of bread or roll at one time.
- DO NOT lick your fingers, lean on the table with your elbows, use your fingers to push food onto your fork (use a knife), take large portions of food you cannot possibly eat, stir or mash food into a heap on your plate, scrape plates at the table or pile them up, talk with food in your mouth, chew with your mouth open, reach across the table for food, get up to reach for food or tip back in your chair.
- DO send a thank-you note to your hostess within a week of his or her hospitality.

American Table Settings

- Generally, plates are set about one inch from the edge of the table. Bread and butter plates go to the left of the dinner plate, above the forks. But if salad is served with the main course, the salad plate often replaces the bread and butter plate at the top left.

- Glasses are placed to the right of the plate above the knife.
- Silverware is placed one inch from the table edge.
- The fork is to the left of the plate, with the fork to be used first on the outside.
- The knife is to the right of the plate—cutting edge facing in. Butter knives, if used, can be placed across the bread-and-butter or salad plate.
- The spoon is to the right of the knife—the spoon used first is on the outside. Never leave a spoon in your cup or glass; after using it, put it on your saucer or your plate, not on the table.
- Napkins can be placed in the center of the plate or to the left of forks. A simple fold has the open corners of an oblong fold at the bottom right.
- Allow 24 inches for each place setting, 30 inches if there is a side plate for bread or salad.

Clothing

A hostess can wear anything she chooses, provided it is in good taste. Some women love to wear the unusual. Be bold—here is an opportunity to get out your long hostess skirt.

Let your guests know whether the occasion is casual or formal or a theme party that requires wearing costumes or seasonal dress.

In some sections of the country, as in the West, I've noticed some men do not remove their cowboy hats even in restaurants. But good manners require that a man remove his hat in the house, when the flag passes by in a street parade, and so on. What I'm saying is, in some locales it is probably not considered bad manners for a man to wear a hat indoors or a woman to wear hair curlers in public, but it still doesn't come across as good manners.

Children

You can teach children courtesy at an early age. One of my friends says that children should be "tamed and trained" by parents investing time with them. Do teach your children not to push in line ahead of others in a cafeteria or at church suppers. Gluttony and a "me first" attitude have no place in the Christian walk.

For the sake of others, please take your crying baby out of a room, a church service or a restaurant until he or she has quieted down.

If you have small children, go out with your husband occasionally without them. I know of a five-year-old who had never been without his mom, and when they enrolled him for the first time in Sunday School, he couldn't manage without her.

Appreciation

Appreciate what others have and enjoy the beauty of their things without being envious. Along the same line, don't hesitate to have someone over who has more material possessions than you do. One young woman groaned, "I'd never have the Martins over, because I don't have fine china dishes, crystal goblets and sterling silverware like they have." Remember that people want to come to our homes simply for Christian love and fellowship.

HOSPITALITY AND TINY TOTS

What's the best way to handle entertaining when you have young children? There are several options:

1. Forget it.
2. Postpone it.
3. Include children the same age as yours.
4. Set an example.

Mary Ann, a 29-year-old mother of three preschoolers, gave up her career as a registered nurse to be a stay-at-home mother. She set up one room in her house as a playroom and often invited other mothers over with their small children, so she could have adult conversation while everyone watched over their children.

She often invited couples with children for dinner. It wasn't unusual to invite three couples, each having three children. Her husband, Ralph, would set up a picnic table in the dining room (with a sheet underneath to catch food spills), so the little ones could eat in the same room with the parents.

Mary Ann was sensitive to her children's needs and her husband's, as well as her own. She taught her youngsters that there were certain times for different things: quiet time, Mommy time, Daddy time. Once a week Ralph took one of the children with him for a ride or a meal out.

Creative Solutions

Even with good ideas and opportunities, some families find problems in certain situations that dictate other solutions. Sensitive hosts may choose to invite only adults and make other arrangements for their own children's care while the party is in progress.

One of our neighbors decided to invite company for dinner once a week while their lively child was only four years old. They discovered that everyone did better if they hired a sitter to entertain their little one and then put her to bed. They regarded their once-a-week "night out at home" as their Christian hospitality ministry as well as their own recreation.

Theresa, mother of two toddlers, had dessert parties timed so that her children were already in bed when guests arrived. Her only apparent problem was when friends popped in unexpectedly. She finally decided to quit apologizing for how the house looked. She told me, "I hope they come to see us, not our house anyway. I straighten the house in the morning, but if the girls get their rooms a bit disordered during play, I've found I don't need to make excuses. Our house just has a lived-in look."

Training

Dr. Richard Dobbins, a Christian minister and licensed psychologist, says that a child not only needs an example to follow, but he also needs instruction. "If there has been little or no instruction, the children will not know what is expected of them much of the time. It's impossible to raise a child with no need for correction."[1]

What better way to teach our children manners and courtesy than by simply making it part of their home life?

Too often we forget that children need to be exposed to good entertaining practices. What better way to teach our children manners and courtesy than by simply making it part of their home life? Dr. Dobbins points out: "Parents need to model for their children the way they want them to live. Children are great imitators. It is much easier for them to do what their parents say if they see their parents do it first."[2]

Four-year-old Lisa watched her mother, Shirley, serve guests so often that she was allowed to be hostess at the children's table whenever company came. Our own children grew socially as they grew physically, because they were included in dinnertime conversation with our guests. Some of our friends became their friends, too—adopted aunts and uncles.

Quinett, Keith and Sherry also grew spiritually from the times we entertained missionaries, pastors and even strangers at our table. One night Keith's eyes got as big as sugar cookies as he listened, fascinated, to a young man who had served a prison term tell us how he had accepted Jesus while behind bars. That story, told firsthand, was imprinted on our children's minds. I know, because they still talk about it years later.

Says Linda Davis Zumbehl in her book *Homebodies*:

One day, when your children are grown and gone, you'll have time for a perfect house. What matters now is not the house, but the home; and not the children's duties, but the children. To every mother of young children who worries herself unnecessarily with trying to do too much, I can only say, "There is an appointed time for everything. And there is a time for every event under heaven" (Eccles. 3:1).[3]

Discovering what works best for you will take a little experimentation. We all need to determine what our individual capabilities are and use them to the best advantage. There are seasons in every life, and in each season we will find ourselves responding hospitably in a different manner.

The time will come when your nest, like mine, will be empty and the children gone from home. Then there will be plenty of time for leisurely dining or more formal entertaining.

Now I love to go visit my grandchildren and see how their parents—my children—respond to the social graces they learned around our table. Frankly, I'm pleasantly surprised that so much sank in. This is a gracious legacy I hope they will pass on to their children.

Notes

1. Richard Dobbins, "Bringing Them Up with Loving Discipline," *Logos Journal* (Sept/Oct 1977), p. 24.
2. Ibid.
3. Linda Davis Zumbehl, *Homebodies* (Springfield, PA: Whitaker House, 1991), p. 20.

The Titus Circle

Older women . . . are to be reverent in their behavior . . . that they may encourage the young women to lve their husbands, to love their children, to be sensible, pure, workers at home, kind, being subject to their own husbands, that the word of God may not be dishonored.

TITUS 2:3-5, *NASB*

As I have traveled this nation for the past two decades, speaking to women's groups, I have come to realize that we have a generation young women who are lacking in home-making and hospitality skills. Many have a deep need to be nurtured, encouraged and accepted and to have a godly woman to hold them accountable in their Christian journey. What they need are spiritual moms—or mentors—whether they are single, married or mothers themselves.

What do I mean by a mentor? Someone who is willing to pass down her knowledge and training to another woman who is less experienced. My definition: *Someone who encourages and equips another for excellence.* Even a young woman can mentor another as long as she meets Paul's qualification as a woman with a lifestyle worthy of respect.

I like Win Couchman's observation: "A mentor is someone further on down the road from you who is going where you want to go and who is willing to give you some light to help you get there."[1]

We are told to "encourage one another and build each other up" (1 Thess. 5:11). The word "encourage" comes from the same Greek word as one of the names of the Holy Spirit—"paraclete," which means "one who comes along-side to help." That's what a godly mentor can do. We must help the younger generation of women reach their full potential.

The word "mentor" is a buzzword in the marketplace today. Big corporations are encouraging employees to spend several hours a month teaching a younger person in the community. Mentoring should be even more important to Christians, for we also have the love of Jesus to share.

Mentoring Examples

A Longtime Encourager

Renee, a mother of six from Titusville, Florida, found her way to the home of Mary Jo Looney every Tuesday for 10 years—there to be fed a delicious breakfast as well as spiritual food. A letter to me from Renee read:

> God brought Mary Jo into my life when my third child was just a baby and I desperately needed the encouragement of an older woman. She became a spiritual mother to me. She has been to me "Jesus with skin on." When I arrived at her doorstep tired and weary from the demands of motherhood, she provided refreshment to my body, soul and spirit. She helped me focus on God's value system. She urged me to remember that each child is God's righteous seed to raise for His glory. I've become a better mother and wife as a result of her godly influence and her words of encouragement.
>
> Her love affair with God has been a long one, and the fruit produced by such a lifestyle has blessed many young women raising families, who draw strength from her faith. I see her influence reaching generations to come as she allows God to touch the hearts of mothers through her.

Some 10 years ago, God impressed Mary Jo to ask the next 10 young women she encountered to come to supper at her house. Seven came and shared their family stories. They giggled over their stories and were relieved to find they weren't alone in their experiences. They had such a good time together that three women volunteered to host a potluck brunch the following month to see if others would enjoy the fellowship as much as they did.

Today 30 to 40 young women still gather once a month to hear teaching from Mary Jo and several other older women who can instruct and encourage them. They also break up into smaller groups to pray for one another before they leave the meeting.

Some of the young women who come are new in the community and in need of a friend. Others have emotional or spiritual needs. There is always someone there who can identify with the hurting one and pray with her about her concerns. New moms bring their babies soon after birth for the others to see, love and pray over.

I think back to when Mary Jo was there for me those many years ago—to share her "Busy Mama" recipes, to encourage me to begin teaching women's classes and to instruct my daughters how to decorate on a shoestring budget. Mary Jo is still there for me across the telephone miles—a cheerleader I've greatly needed on some days. She hasn't missed sending me a birthday card in 30 years.[2]

Another Busy Mentor

Although Jane Hansen is a very busy woman who serves as

CEO and president of Aglow International—a ministry outreach to women in more than 145 nations—she was so concerned about the need for younger women to be discipled by older Christian women that she decided to mentor a group of young women in her own home one night a month. Even though she travels the world, she still finds time for her at-home ministry night.

When Jane began to plan for the group, she made a guest list of young women she knew who were between the ages of 19 and 35, including her own daughter. Some were married, some were single, and some of the married ones had children, as did some of the single women. Some were Christians; some were not. She wanted to provide a setting that was open and safe for the young women to share their hearts and she desired that each one feel loved and cared about. She provides a meal, decorations, a warm atmosphere and a sharing time so that each young woman feels welcomed and accepted.

Jane realized that some women felt uncomfortable when asked to pray or to look up verses in the Bible, so she brought several simple Bible studies and let the women pick the ones they would like to study. The workbook questions provide a springboard for them to share.

"We've had some very poignant times when the young women poured out their hurts, fears and frustrations," she says. "But they have found acceptance, affirmation and the unconditional love so necessary to the healing process. We've dealt with very real issues such as unfulfilling marriages, unplanned pregnancies, dysfunctional relationships and the pain these situations cause."[3]

On some evenings the focus is on practical helps such as homemaking skills, decorating ideas or makeup tips. Jane tries to be a helpful teacher for whatever the subject the young women are interested in. She's been mentoring her group now for six years in her home.

PERSONAL EXPERIENCES

I've had several occasions to mentor one-on-one as well as to mentor on a regular basis several in a group setting in my home.

Lucy, a young mother of four, was one of the first; and I didn't even know her beforehand. She had heard me speak on the ABCs of hospitality to a women's group.

"May I come to your house to see how a real home should look?" she asked. "I need help and ideas. I don't even know how to set a table properly. With nine kids in our family, we had to take turns eating and only had jars for glasses. Mother didn't teach us any social skills, and I've felt handicapped all my married life." I invited Lucy to come the next Monday.

When I showed her through our house, I pointed out inexpensive ways to decorate on a budget—frame greeting cards and use things already on hand for wall hangings (such as china plates, a quilt, a matted and framed lace doilie). I gave her my favorite "quick to make" recipes, many of them passed on to me years earlier by older women in my church.

It really freed her when she realized I didn't have fancy china or expensive silverware; I use plain white dishes but have a variety of colorful tablecloths made from sheets. And many of my furniture pieces are hand-me-downs or garage-sale purchases.

"People want to come to a home because of its warmth, not for the decor or the food; they come for the love," I told her. Inch by inch Lucy grew in her confidence and ability until finally at her husband's urging she was ready to open her home for a weekly Bible study. Whenever she felt discouraged, she would call and ask me to pray with her. I kept up with her for years, either by letter or phone, as she and her family moved to other locales.

Once when I had a mentoring group of young single Christian women, I made up a workbook list we used for several months. This helped them to be disciplined and accountable. I used the original version of this book as our textbook, having them read and study one chapter at a time.

Since "older women are to . . . encourage the young women," I first set my own goals as a mentor. (In addition to these goals, see appendix C for a full description of the plan I use for the young single group I mentor.)

- Help the young women discover their life-purpose (see Luke 1:38; Eph. 2:10).
- Encourage and equip them to live for God's glory.
- Pray for them individually according to their needs and goals.

- Teach them some homemaking skills and hospitality helps (such as how to set the table, make tablecloths from decorator sheets, create a beautiful centerpiece using what they already have, etc.)
- Get other women to help me when the group has an interest in learning something I am not skilled at doing.
- Answer any questions that arise. If I don't know the answers, I will find someone who does.
- Let them occasionally reciprocate by planning a meal we can enjoy together at someone's home other than mine.[4]

The Holy Spirit can teach us through Scripture and encourage us when we are discouraged. But when God provides a mentor to speak into our lives on a regular basis, it seems easier knowing that an encouraging person is just a telephone call away. It's also actually a comfort to be accountable to someone more mature in the Lord.

It's actually a comfort to be accountable to someone more mature in the Lord.

As you reflect on your life, no doubt you will recall certain women who have taught you practical and spiritual principles. Have you, on the other hand, had an opportunity to train—or mentor—some younger women?

Older women sometimes feel threatened by the younger generation, and the younger feel intimidated by the older. This ought not to be, yet I'm afraid it is, even in Christian circles. If there is a skill you want to learn, find an older or more accomplished woman (whatever her chronological age) and ask her to teach you that skill. Nothing is more flattering to a gifted person than for someone to share her interest.

The apostle Paul said: "Do nothing out of selfish ambition or vain conceit, but in humility consider others better than yourselves. Each of you should look not only to your own interests, but also to the interests of others" (Phil. 2:3-4).

When you find a gracious Christian woman blessed in the skills you need to develop, ask her "Will you 'Titus' me?" If she's in tune with the Holy Spirit, she will find time and ways to help you. But don't be disappointed if the only one you want is too committed at the moment to include you in her schedule. She may find time later. In the meantime, ask God for another woman who is not as busy.

BIBLICAL MENTORING

In biblical times a daughter often married at an early age and the mother-in-law stepped in to continue the training the girl's own mother had begun. Daughter-in-law and mother-in-law usually developed a deep and continuing bond.

Have you ever imagined the mentoring that went on—woman to woman—in the Bible accounts? Naomi repeatedly referred to her daughter-in-law Ruth as "my daughter" and we know she taught her about spiritual things. Ruth stuck by her when Naomi decided as a widow to return to her Israelite people. "Your people will be my people and your God my God," Ruth told her. Naomi instructed and trained Ruth after their return to Israel. Later, through her marriage to Boaz, Ruth became a part of the lineage of Christ (see Ruth 1:1-16; 4-13-22).

Think of Elizabeth, while pregnant with John the Baptist, mentoring her younger cousin, the virgin Mary, who awaited the birth of the Messiah she carried in her womb. These two women relatives rejoiced and praised God for His goodness to them in their time spent together (see Luke 1:35-56).

Lois was a woman who instilled spiritual truths into her daughter Eunice, who had a son named Timothy. Together, grandmother and mother had an impact on this young evangelist whom Paul highly treasured as one who would later carry on his ministry (see 2 Tim. 1:5).

Dorcas, a well-known seamstress, was resurrected after her untimely death through the prayers of Peter, because her ministry was so needed (see Acts 9:36-42). Ever thought of all the others she might have mentored—or taught to sew?

FULL CIRCLE

I am forever thankful for the women who had an input in my life, though I probably didn't appreciate their efforts at the time as much as I do now. Recently I had a chance to thank them personally.

After a 20-year absence, I was invited to my old church as their women's retreat speaker. What an honor! This was the church full of women who had mentored me when I was a mom with three young children.

I realized I had come full circle—now I was a grandmother coming to encourage a younger generation of women who love the Lord. I was plenty nervous yet excited.

At the last session, as I spoke on hospitality and mentoring, I was surrounded by a few cherished best friends from years ago. During my speech, I paid them tribute and asked each woman to stand as I told what she had imparted to my life. Mary Jo had been my mentor for many years following that day she came to decorate my house. Margaret made my curtains and taught me and my daughter to bake bread. Lib prayed faithfully with me on the phone every weekday morning for 17 years. Barbara had stood in some tough prayer gaps with me. Liz, owner of a flower boutique, had tried to teach me to arrange bouquets but was mostly my "let's have some fun" friend.

After I sat down and lunch was about to be served, a young woman came to our table and asked to speak to all of us older women. She said, "When we younger women, sitting at my table, heard how you have been friends all these years—even when one of you moved away—and how you have continued to pray for one another, it touched us all. We made a covenant today to do the same. We want to have lifelong friendships like you have, and we want to pray for each other, too. Thank you for a great show-and-tell lesson." Most of us "oldies" shed a tear or two.[5]

Yes, I had come full circle—the Titus circle!

Notes

1. Win Couchman, quoted in Dee Brestin, *The Friendships of Women* (Wheaton, IL: Victor Books, 1989), p. 162.
2. Quin Sherrer and Ruthanne Garlock, *A Woman's Guide to Getting Through Tough Times* (Ann Arbor, MI: Servant Publications, 1998), pp. 202-203.
3. Jane Hansen, "Let's Talk," *Connection Newsletter* (winter 1995), p. 2.
4. Quin Sherrer and Ruthanne Garlock, *A Woman's Guide to Spirit-Filled Living* (Ann Arbor, MI: Servant Publications, 1996), pp. 98-99.
5. Quin Sherrer, *Good Night, Lord* (Ventura, CA: Regal Books, 2000), pp. 241-242.

A Plan for Bible Study

A study of the Word of God gives us plenty of examples of the importance of being hospitable. But along with Bible study, we need to find practical ways to be hospitable that fit our individual lifestyles, budgets and schedules. You will probably notice that with each season of your life, your expression of hospitality will change too.

The following questions and suggested Scripture studies are a springboard to get you started on your road to hospitality. Later in the appendix there will be questions specific to each chapter in this book. But the first few pages are more general in scope. You can cover in one sitting as much or as little of the material as is comfortable for you. But please take the time to look up all the Scripture passages to get a complete picture of what the Bible says about hospitality and the importance of opening our homes to others.

All of the questions and Scripture studies can be used for individual or group study, or as part of a mentoring program. The studies are not exhaustive; most likely you will think of many other ideas to add to the ones in this book as you search the Scriptures or talk to your friends who are experiencing the delight of extending hospitality. May you know the joy of showing God's kindness to others without hesitation.

You will need a Bible, a Bible concordance, a notebook and a pen. Ready to get started?

A GENERAL STUDY ON HOSPITALITY

The practice of hospitality must be very important to God because it is one of the qualifications listed for Church elders (see 1 Tim. 3:2). In the New Testament, the Greek word translated as "hospitality" literally means "love of strangers." In the Old Testament, extending hospitality toward strangers and the poor was strongly encouraged (see Lev.19:33-34; 25:14-15,23).

There are many Scriptures that encourage us to be hospitable, including, "Cheerfully share your home with those who need a meal or a place to stay for the night" (1 Pet. 4:9, *TLB*) Maybe you have never looked at your home as a ministry tool, but now you are wanting to explore that avenue.

Perhaps one of the best biblical examples of practicing hospitality is found in Acts 2:42,46-47: Right after the outpouring of the Holy Spirit on the Day of Pentecost, believers began meeting together to devote themselves to four things:

- the apostles' teaching
- fellowship
- breaking of bread
- prayer

Notice that they not only went to the Temple, but their homes also became small sanctuaries, or temples, for teaching, prayer, fellowship and meals.

Have you considered being part of a group of Christians who meet in a home where teaching, prayer, fellowship and breaking of bread is a usual happening? Have you asked God if He wants your home opened for such a meeting? To learn more about the fellowship of believers, read the following Scriptures for study and reflection: Acts 2:42, 46-47; Acts 12:12; Acts 16:14-15,40; Acts 21:8,16; Romans 16:3-5.

Read Leviticus 19:34a; Psalm 37:26; Romans 12:13; Hebrews 13:16; 1 Peter 4:9-11. What conclusions can be drawn about hospitality from these Scriptures?

NEW TESTAMENT HOSPITALITY

Jesus enjoyed going to the home of Martha and Mary in Bethany more than anywhere else in Judea. They made Him feel welcomed and loved. Scripture records one of the main incidents in this Bethany home when Martha served Him and Mary sat at His feet. We need to be both a Mary and a Martha, sitting first in His presence and then serving others.

What did Jesus caution Martha about? Read Luke 10:38-42. Look up the definition of "distracted" or "distraction" to see how it might apply to your life today. Ask God how you can bring balance to a busy schedule.

By serving others we are following Jesus and doing what He commands. Think about the importance of serving others after reading Mark 10:45; Luke 22:27; John 13:14.

Consider how the word "hospitality" is applied in the following Scriptures: Romans 12:13; Romans 16:23; 1 Timothy 5:10; 1 Peter 4:9; 3 John 8. What general principle have you gleaned from what you have just read?

Far-Reaching Effects of Hospitality
Aquila and Priscilla were a husband-wife team whose hospitality had far-reaching effects on the Early Church. Read about how they hosted Paul as their guest in Corinth (see

Acts 18:2-3). Note their continued hospitality to Apollos (see Acts 18:26) and how Apollos went on to help other believers (see Acts 18:27-28). Often the people you bless through hospitality will bless others, too.

Paul also wrote to the church at Philippi about a brother in the Lord—Epaphroditus—and how to treat him (read Phil. 2:25-30). Can you think of anyone like him to whom you could minister?

When you read 3 John 5-8, you will discover that John compliments those who were faithful in their hospitality to strangers, sending them on their way in a manner worthy of God.

In the Early Church there was a mixture of races, religious backgrounds and social classes—Jews, barbarians, Greeks, slaves, free men, rich, poor. Jews sometimes looked down on Gentile brothers and vice versa. Paul had to tell them, "Welcome and receive [to your hearts] one another, then, even as Christ has welcomed and received you, for the glory of God" (Rom. 15:7, *AMP*).

Some of the more obscure and easy-to-overlook examples of hospitality in the New Testament have the most to teach us about hospitality. Why not look up what the Scriptures have to say about the following people and their hospitality acts. Study them for yourself.

- Simon the tanner: He provided Peter with lodging and food while in Joppa, meaning that Simon's home became Peter's while he was there ministering (see Acts 10:5-6).

- Cornelius: This Roman centurion had a vision and sent for Peter to come to inform him about the ways of Jesus. Cornelius, along with his relatives and close friends, believed in Christ; and the Holy Spirit was poured out on Gentiles for the first time (see Acts 10:9-48)
- Mary, the mother of John (also called Mark): Mary was hosting a powerful prayer meeting in her home when Peter was miraculously released from prison by an angel. He made his way immediately to her house to share his good news with the astonished believers who were still praying (see Acts 12:1-16).
- Lydia: This prosperous businesswoman opened her heart to respond to Paul's message about Jesus, then she and her household were baptized. Immediately she invited Paul and his friends into her home. After Paul and Silas came out of prison, they went to Lydia's house where brothers in the Lord met and encouraged them. Surely hers was a house of meeting, refuge and peace (see Acts 16:13-15, 40).
- Paul's Philippian jailer: This man was on the verge of suicide after an earthquake that caused the prison doors to come free provided escape for the prisoners he was guarding; instead of harming himself, he was persuaded by Paul to believe in Jesus and receive eternal life—along with his whole household. The jailer brought Paul and Silas to his

home for a meal (see Acts 16:27-34).

- Philip: This man, one of the original seven deacons and an evangelist, opened his Caesarea home to Paul and Luke while they were in the vicinity (see Acts 21:8).

- Mnason of Cyrus: This man provided lodging for Paul, Luke and some of the disciples from Caesarea when they were near Jerusalem. This may well have meant opening his home to Gentile believers as well as to Jews, which would have taken great courage during this time of persecution of Christians (see Acts 21:16).

- Phoebe: Paul instructed the believers in Rome to care for the needs of Phoebe "in a way worthy of the saints," because this visiting Christian sister had been a helper of many, including Paul (Rom. 16:2).

- Gaius: This man was commended by Paul for allowing Paul and the whole church in Corinth to enjoy his hospitality (see Rom. 16:23).

- Philemon: He must have been a cordial host, because Paul felt free to invite himself to stay with him (see Philem. 22).

Other Scriptures that speak of hospitality include Luke 14:13-14; Romans 12:13; 1 Timothy 3:2; 5:10; Titus 1:8; 1 Peter 4:9. Write a couple of paragraphs about what the Lord is saying to you through these verses on extending hospitality.

Jesus' Teaching on Hospitality

The Lord Jesus illustrates hospitality in the story about the good Samaritan (see Luke 10:30-37). He promises to reward hospitality and regards its service toward His disciples in the same way as service toward Himself.

He also emphasized the importance of hospitality by answering the question of who should inherit the Kingdom: "I was a stranger and you invited me in" (Matt. 25:35).

Read and reflect on Matthew 10:40-42:

He who receives you receives me, and he who receives me receives the one who sent me. Anyone who receives a prophet because he is a prophet will receive a prophet's reward, and anyone who receives a righteous man because he is righteous man will receive a righteous man's reward. And if anyone gives even a cup of cold water to one of these little ones because he is my disciple, I tell you the truth, he will certainly not lose his reward.

Describe how your life would be different if you applied these verses at every opportunity. Then tell one thing you could do today to give "a cup of cold water" to someone?

Old Testament Hospitality

Abraham

Consideration of others seems to have been in God's plan from the beginning. When Abraham encountered his three special guests sent from God, he eagerly greeted them and offered hospitality. We read in Genesis 18:1-7 how Abraham

- hurried to meet them;
- had water brought to wash their tired, dirty feet;
- offered them rest under his tree;
- invited them to stay and eat a meal.

He then rushed into his tent and instructed Sarah to make some bread while he picked a choice calf for his servant to prepare for their unexpected guests.

Abraham was expressing good manners and offering hospitality in a typical Middle Eastern fashion. Notice that although the husband directed the hospitality, it was actually a joint effort, as the most gracious hospitality always is.

The *Encyclopedia Judaica* has this to say about biblical hospitality:

> The Bible is replete with examples of pious hospitality. As soon as Abraham saw the three men of Mamre "from afar," he hurried to invite them into his house, ministered to their physical comfort, and served them lavishly (Gen. 18). Similarly, Laban was eager to welcome Abraham's servant (Gen. 24:28-32) while Rebekah attended to the comfort of his camels. . . . Manoah did not allow the angel to depart before he had partaken of his hospitality (Judges 13:15). . . . David repaid a courtesy which Barzillai had extended to his men (2 Sam. 17:27-29)

with a courtesy to Barzillai's servant Chimham (2 Sam. 19:32-40).[1]

Other Old Testament Examples

Read 1 Samuel 25:14-35. Abigail's hospitality to David and his men not only provided them with food, but her act also prevented bloodshed. Are there other lessons here the Lord wants to speak to you about?

Read about Elisha and the Shunammite woman who made a room for the holy man of God to stay in when he came by (2 Kings 4:8-36). She too experienced a miracle. What was it?

Read the story about the widow in 1 Kings 17:7-24. What did she discover when she rendered hospitality to Elijah?

For further examples of how the Bible encourages hospitality to strangers and the poor, see Genesis 19:1-3; Exodus 2:20; Leviticus 19:33-34; Deuteronomy 15:7-11; Judges 13:15-16; Judges 19:16-21; Ruth 2.

Note

1. *Encyclopedia Judaica*, Vol. 8 (Jerusalem Israel: Keter Publishing House, 1972), p. 1031

A Study Guide for This Book

Chapter One: A Welcoming Home

1. Who are the most important people to receive your hospitality? Why?
2. How can you improve your hospitality to them? Ask God to give you wisdom and write down what He shows you.

3. What is your dinner-table conversation like? How could it be improved?

4. How do you, as the woman of the house, set the mood in your home for your family? When you have guests?

5. What could you do to make family or guests feel even more special?

Have you asked Jesus to help you accept your home and turn it into a haven for your family? If not, you should do so now. Try writing a prayer, thanking God for your home and the opportunity to be hospitable. To get you started, here's an example of one of my prayers:

Lord, thank You for my home. Help me not be concerned about the sheer physical strength it takes to bring order out of chaos. I do love this house. I leave it in Your care tonight as I fall asleep in Your peace. Lord, bless the friends who are coming to share our hospitality. May it be a special time for them and for us. Let me be less concerned about the way things look and more concerned about how You want me to serve our guests. May I be a blessing to them, and may they be a blessing to me. I ask in Jesus' name. Amen.[1]

Chapter 2: A Dream House on a Tight Budget

Have you been pining for a dream house instead of turning the one you have into a comfortable, peaceful dwelling?

1. What are some practical ways you could make your house into a dream home?

2. Have you considered asking friends to come help you clean house, rearrange furniture and give you their decorating ideas? Why not help each other by taking turns working at each other's homes? It's great fun when you have three or four people involved.

3. What does your master bedroom look like? Messy? Cluttered? How could you turn it into a quiet refuge?

4. What would it take to get your house in order? What cleaning task would give you the most satisfaction to have out of the way? What kind of plan or schedule would allow you to tackle that one housecleaning job today or within the week?

5. Are you a perfectionist? One woman told me her family room was so perfect she never let the family use it. Are there ways that you need to be less demanding and more understanding of the clutter of daily living? In what ways could you let your family enjoy their living space more?

6. What does God says about order, peace and the times and seasons of life? (see Eccles. 3:6; Isa. 32:18; 1 Cor.14:40)

7. Read Numbers 6:24-26; Deuteronomy 6:5-6,9; 20:5; Psalm 30; Matthew 10:12-13; Revelation 3:20. If you have not dedicated your home to the Lord, try writing a dedication ceremony, based on

these verses, and make the occasion of reading the dedication a celebration with family and friends as you give your home to the Lord.

Chapter 3: A Balance Between Giving and Receiving

1. Read Romans 15:7 and write out what you think it means to receive one another just as Christ received us.
2. Make a study of some of the reciprocal pronouns in the New Testament. You can find these in a concordance under the words "one another." Let God speak to you about some of these commands as they apply to hospitality, sharing and caring.
3. Scripture commands, and the Holy Spirit commissions, every believer to be concerned about caring for one another. Look up Ephesians 4:12 and 1 Peter 4:10 in *The Living Bible* (an easy-to-read paraphrase). Ask God to show you what special abilities you have to help equip God's people. Are you willing to use them? How would you use them? Where?

Chapter 4: Open-Door Blessings

If, in the past, you haven't opened your home to others, how could you begin to extend hospitality in various ways? In what ways could you allow your children or your husband to become more involved in these areas of hospitality? Perhaps you might consider inviting your husband's friends from work, or even your children's friends, over for a meal with your family? Pray about the people God wants you to invite to sit at your table. (Don't go against your husband's wishes if he is against inviting guests.)

To be better prepared for hospitality how can you

- do your shopping and planning?
- arrange your dining area?
- adapt your sleeping and bath accommodations?
- create peaceful surroundings for your guests?
- enjoy your guests without worrying about the many preparations?
- prepare a menu you feel comfortable cooking?
- find time to soak your house in prayer?
- encourage your family to become involved?
- learn how not to be stressed out when company's coming?

Chapter 5: Keepers of the Inn
Have you thought through how you would treat an overnight guest or one who stayed several days in your home? Here are some questions to get you thinking about your own style of caring for guests.

1. Have you considered that all guests should be received as Christ in your home? Do you need to make any attitude adjustments in this regard?

2. What difference is there between entertaining and hospitality?

3. What are some of the do-nots of hospitality? What are some of the ways to bless your guests?

4. Can you think of other personal tips on how to bless a guest?

5. Do you consider yourself a flexible person? If not, how can you come to that place in life?

6. Are you able to maintain a sense of humor when things go awry? Once a luncheon guest accidentally knocked over the card table at a friend's home, sending four expensive china plates crashing to the floor. My friend, more concerned about her guest's feelings than her plates, graciously smoothed over her guest's embarrassment. How would you have reacted to such an incident?

7. In *The Living Bible*, read Proverbs 31 about the virtuous woman and note some of the qualities described, which you may already exhibit (perhaps you are one who looks for bargains). Brainstorm more ways you can identify with this woman's description without feeling guilty or less than.

8. Are there any questionable objects, not God-honoring, that you need to remove from your home?

9. How can you make family and guests feel more special in the way you treat them?

10. What character traits are your weakest ones? Remember that with God's help, you can improve.

How about patience, cleanliness, cooking, gossip? Look up Scriptures that go with these issues and memorize them, asking God to help you overcome the areas where you are weak.

11. What are some practical hints to bless your family? Do they look forward to special traditions each year? Could you start some new traditions? Share your thoughts with your family and get their ideas.

Chapter 6: Angels and Strangers

Read Hebrews 13:2. Have you or someone you know ever had such an experience? If you are studying these questions with a group, share your experience with them.

1. Have you had opportunity to be hospitable to strangers? What, if anything, would you do differently now from when you had that opportunity?
2. When the doorbell or the phone rings, what is your attitude when you answer? Have you viewed these "interruptions" as opportunities from the Lord to show His courtesy through you?
3. List some ways you can be hospitable to singles, a widow or widower, a college student or a neighbor. It won't always be convenient to help someone. One of my friends has a neighbor who calls her without prior notice, often to drive her to the doctor's office. How would you respond to such unplanned requests?

4. If you can't have guests in your home, think of other ways you can be hospitable in this particular period of your life. Is there a neighbor you can invite to lunch? Do you know a harried mom for whom you could baby-sit? Do you know an invalid whom you could visit or whose house you could clean?

Chapter 7: A Gracious Legacy

Do your manners need sharpening up? Remember, practice makes perfect.

1. In what social skills would you like to be more proficient?
2. Have you considered practicing setting the table when no one is looking? Or observing a friend who has more expertise? Are you too proud to ask a friend to come teach you?
3. What could you teach another woman about good manners (if she asks you)?
4. How can you still be hospitable if you have tiny tots? Or how can you express hospitality to someone who has small children? Ask God for creative ways to be show hospitality and record your ideas in your notebook.
5. Have you discovered what works best for your family at this season of your life? Have you taught your children to be hospitable? Have you put off having guests until the children leave the nest?

6. What could you do right now to begin practicing hospitality?

Chapter 8: The Titus Circle

Consider your God-given qualities that could be used to encourage the life of someone else. Thank Him for your uniqueness and ask Him to stir up creativity in you.

1. What is your definition of a mentor?
2. Have you ever had a mentor? If so, what was the most important thing she taught you?
3. Have you written thank-you letters to the older women who have influenced or impacted your life? List these people and then find ways to show them your appreciation.
4. Is there someone you need to encourage, to teach, to come alongside to help develop her potential more fully?
5. Think of other women you know who could teach you some skills you have always wanted to learn. Perhaps you could barter one of your talents with one of these women and let her also glean from your life.

Note

1. Quin Sherrer, *Good Night, Lord* (Ventura, CA: Regal Books, 2000), p. 46.

A Guide for Mentoring

If you are mentoring a group of young singles, you may want to use some of these questions and instructions I wrote for an eight-week mentoring class I once taught. Adapt these as necessary, write them out and give the pages to each young woman to work through during the duration of your meetings.

1. Write out your life verse from the Bible—the verse that means the most to you and daily guides your steps.

2. Write out your life's goal. Be specific, not "religious." (For example, I always wanted to be a wife, mother and writer.)

3. What are you doing right now to achieve that goal? Are you taking night classes, learning to play an instrument, studying a foreign language?

4. Do you have some close friends your own age with whom you can pray on a regular basis?

5. Do you have a problem with worry, or anxiety? With weight? Whatever your weak area, find at least three Bible verses that speak to that situation and memorize them. (For example, if your weak area is worry, you should find several instances when Jesus said "Do not be anxious." To worry is a distraction; it is not trusting God to meet your needs.)

6. How do other people view you? What image do you portray? Do you have a good self-image or a sloppy don't-care one?

7. Would you like help in learning some skills (how to bake bread, apply makeup, organize your bedroom closet, make your bedroom more attractive and less messy, etc.) you haven't yet developed and, if so, have you considered which older woman in your church could help teach you?

8. Are you disciplined in your prayer life and Bible reading? Set realistic goals for a devotional time with the Lord. For example, to make time for prayer, you could plan to get up 10 minutes earli-

er each morning the first week and then 15 minutes the next week. Before long you will have increased this time, which will become such a special way to begin your day.

9. What are some of your priorities right now?

10. Get a separate notebook that only you and God will read and get real honest with your heavenly Father about these areas in your life: (*a*) your weaknesses, (*b*) your strengths, (*c*) the wisest use of your gifts and talents and (*d*) people against whom you hold grudges because of past hurts and disappointments. Choose to forgive them, so God can unchain (loose) you from that bondage and hear your prayers (see Mark 11:22-26). Pour out your heart to the Lord, praying Scripture, listing your dreams, hopes and anything else you might want to talk to God about. Make it truthful and personal. Write down any thoughts or directions He gives you and record the date, so you can later go back to that note and see how He answered your prayers. Please don't presume that God is going to answer your prayer in your time frame or your expected way. Wait with faith but not with presumption.

A Mentoring Relationship

When you enter a mentoring relationship, there must be a mutual understanding from the start. Here are some of the issues to agree on and some standards to set.

- Decide when and how often you will get together. This usually is weekly or monthly.
- Be committed to a schedule and ask for a commitment (some women write a statement committing to meet for a set time period and both parties sign it).
- Discuss your goals for mentoring. Ask your partner for her input and what she wants to get out of your time together.
- Will you mentor one-on-one or meet with several women at a time?
- Decide which study books you will use (Bible version and workbook or study guide).
- Pray daily for the person you are mentoring, but also ask her to get a prayer partner.
- Encourage her to keep some type of journal of what she is learning and what God is showing her.
- Teach her in such a way that she can begin to teach others.
- Remember that your hope is that your disciple will take your ideas and build on them, going even beyond you, the mentor.[1]

Note

1. Quin Sherrer and Ruthanne Garlock, *A Woman's Guide to Spirit-Filled Living* (Ann Arbor, MI: Servant Publications, 1996), pp. 98-99.

Recommended Reading

Biehl, Bobb. *Mentoring.* Nashville, TN: Broadman and Holman, 1996. Encouragement to find a mentor and become one.

Greig, Doris W. *We Didn't Know They Were Angels.* Ventura, CA: Regal Books, 1987. Inspiration to practice hospitality, even when it's inconvenient. Includes family-tested recipes.

Hagee, Diane. *The King's Daughter.* Nashville, TN: Thomas Nelson, 2001. A delightful book about how older women in a church congregation can successfully touch the lives of younger women through mentoring classes.

———. *Not By Bread Alone*. San Antonio, TX: John Hagee Ministries, n.d. A guide to creative ministry through food. Includes time-tested recipes.

Hansen, Jane. *Where Hearts Are Shared*. Ventura, CA: Regal Books, 2001. Offers simple recipes and tips on entertaining from women around the world.

Hunt, Susan. *Spiritual Mothering*. Wheaton, IL: Crossway Books, 1992. Describes the Titus 2 model for women mentoring women.

Kraft, Vickie. *Women Mentoring Women*. Chicago: Moody Press, 1991. Describes ways to start, maintain and expand a biblical women's ministry.

Kreider, Larry. *The Cry for Spiritual Fathers and Mothers*. Ephrata, PA: House to House Publications, 2000. Why we desperately need to have spiritual fathers and mothers mentoring those within the Church.

Platz, Ann and Wales, Susan. *Social Graces*. Eugene, OR: Harvest House Publishers, 1999. A guide to manners, conversation and charm for today.

Schaeffer, Edith. *Hidden Art*. Wheaton, IL: Tyndale House Publishers, 1975. Inspiration to use your home and talents for the glory of God.

Sherrer, Quin, and Garlock, Ruthanne. *How to Pray for Your Children*. Ventura, CA: Regal Books, 1998. A guide to praying for your children from birth to adulthood; includes baby dedication service and ways to bless your family in a home setting.

———. *Praying Prodigals Home*. Ventura, CA: Regal Books, 2000. Some of our loved ones alienated from God may be reached by our unconditional love and hospitality.

———. *Prayers Women Pray*. Ann Arbor, MI: Servant Publications, 1998. Intimate moments with God for every occasion and season of a woman's life.

Sherrer, Quin. *Good Night, Lord*. Ventura, CA: Regal Books, 1999. Quin's prayer journal details her experiences as a mom and in the realm of hospitality.

Sims, Barbara. *Homemade Hospitality*. Uhrichsville, OH: Barbour Publishing, 2001. Practical pointers and unique low-cost ideas to help you rediscover the joy of hospitality.

Van Atta, Lucibel. *Women Encouraging Women: Who Will Disciple Me?* Portland, OR: Multnomah Press, 1987. A practical guide from a mature woman who has mentored younger women for years.

ENRICH YOUR LIFE

**We Didn't Know
They Were Angels**
Discovering the Gift
of Christian Hospitality
Doris W. Greig
Paperback
ISBN 08307.13352

**Where Hearts Are Shared
Cookbook**
Simple Recipes and Tips for
Entertaining from Women
Around The World
Jane Hansen
Hardcover
ISBN 08307.28937

**Women: God's
Secret Weapon**
God's Inspiring Message
to Women of Power,
Purpose and Destiny
Ed Silvoso
Paperback
ISBN 08307.28872

First Place
The Bible's Way
to Weight Loss
Carole Lewis
with *Terry Whalin*
Hardcover
ISBN 08307.28635

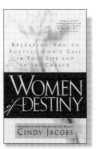

Women of Destiny
Releasing You to Fulfill
God's Call in Your Life
and in the Church
Cindy Jacobs
Paperback
ISBN 08307.18648

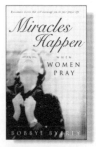

**Miracles Happen
When Women Pray**
Eyewitness Stories That
Will Encourage You
in Your Prayer Life
Bobbye Byerly
Paperback
ISBN 08307.26462

Regal
FROM GOSPEL LIGHT

Available at your local Christian bookstore.
www.regalbooks.com